AN INQUIRY, ETC.

AN INQUIRY
INTO
THE CONDITION AND PROSPECTS
OF THE
AFRICAN RACE
IN THE
UNITED STATES

By
An American Of The
District Of Columbia, June, 1839.

The Black Heritage Library Collection

BOOKS FOR LIBRARIES PRESS
FREEPORT, NEW YORK
1971

First Published 1839
Reprinted 1971

LIBRARY
FLORIDA STATE UNIVERSITY
TALLAHASSEE, FLORIDA

Reprinted from a copy in the
Fisk University Library Negro Collection

INTERNATIONAL STANDARD BOOK NUMBER:
0-8369-8790-X

LIBRARY OF CONGRESS CATALOG CARD NUMBER:
70-154079

PRINTED IN THE UNITED STATES OF AMERICA

AN INQUIRY

INTO

THE CONDITION AND PROSPECTS

OF THE

AFRICAN RACE

IN THE

United States:

AND

THE MEANS OF BETTERING ITS FORTUNES.

"Indignantly frown upon the first dawning of every attempt to alien any portion of our country from the rest."—GEORGE WASHINGTON.

BY AN AMERICAN.

PHILADELPHIA:
HASWELL, BARRINGTON, AND HASWELL.
1839.

ENTERED according to the Act of Congress, in the year 1839, by HASWELL, BARRINGTON, and HASWELL, in the Clerk's Office of the District Court of the Eastern District of Pennsylvania.

CONTENTS.

INTRODUCTION . . . . . . PAGE 13

CHAPTER I.

TO NORTHERN ABOLITIONISTS.

I. Why first appeal to Abolitionists—result of their measures doubtful.—Writer, once an abolitionist—how cured.
II. Ultraism of the present day—in theology—and benevolence.
III. Writer's views of slavery—caused by man's depravity—no remedy but Christianity—moral influence of our national prosperity.—Coronation of England's queen—Dr. Franklin.
IV. Circumstances in which slavery may be a blessing—theory and practice of abolitionists inconsistent—reference to St. Paul—objections to holding slaves.

V. Action and measures of abolitionists, why wrong—abolition periodicals—Mr. Garrison—editor in New York—should be judged charitably.

VI. Slaveholders' ideas of abolitionists—why—many slave-owners anxious to get rid of slavery—what abolitionists ought to have done—arguments not admitted—abolitionists seriously questioned.

VII. Abolition in District of Columbia opposed—why? p. 21

CHAPTER II.

APPEAL TO SLAVEHOLDERS.

I. Design of the writer. Slaveholders and abolitionists ignorant of each other.

II. Character of abolitionists misunderstood — enthusiasts—increased by opposition—many of them well-meaning men.

III. Slavery, general view—negroes human beings, capable of improvement.

IV. Power of the master — slaveholders interrogated. Fearful responsibility in holding human beings as slaves.

V. The Bible on that responsibility.

VI. Brief survey of practical slavery—moral aspect—ignorance —dishonesty, facts in proof—licentiousness, slaveholders aware of the evil.

CONTENTS. 9

VII. Influence of slavery on individuals—character of slaves—their influence on masters—on poor white men.

VIII. Influence of slavery on national prosperity—monopoly of cotton—southern system not favourable to improvement—comparison with imperial Rome—with Peru and Mexico.

IX. A better system recommended to the South. Question of moral right will be agitated among slaveholders.

X. Slaveholders plead that a manufacturing country makes actual slaves—some weight in the plea—radical difference. Southern states should depend on agriculture. " Plan " of independence considered.

XI. Views of the North on slavery—tendency of abolition—ridiculous action among some northern manufacturers.

XII. Dissolution of Union threatened—its preservation urged upon the South. North not inimical to the South.

XIII. The probable result of the controversy. Influence of British emancipation. Modern slavery compared with Roman and Grecian. Conclusion . . . . . p. 63

CHAPTER III.

TO THE FREE STATES.

I. Free and slave states diametrically opposed—what influence this should exert on the former—why oppose the spirit of abolition—how the South may be reached.

II. Why slaveholders should be judged charitably—and the subject investigated—northern ministers appealed to—northern men at the South—severe taskmasters—why.

III. Power of habit, the stronghold of slavery, influence of filial and venerable associations among slaveholders—opposed to unconditional emancipation—why.

IV. Universal conviction of the right of property.—Value of slaves.—Ignorance of northern men respecting slavery.

V. Condition of the slave—observations of the writer—house servants many advantages—field labourers—negro houses—bad—mode of feeding slaves—various resources among them—public opinion in favour of humanity—dress of slaves—personal treatment—mode of labour—general appearance and manners—many of them in places of trust—general views of the whites—influence of the age on the slave.

VI. Free blacks of the South—situation unfavourable to improvement—interesting exceptions.

VII. Condition of the free blacks at the North—anecdote—degraded—outcasts—vicious—neglected by the whites—deep-rooted prejudice against them—proofs—what justice requires of the free states.—North not guiltless respecting slavery—what atonement for her own wrongs.

VIII. South devoted to the Union.—Interference of the North, on the question of moral right—appeal to the free states—to the clergy—examine motives—forbearance recommended among equals—injurious effects of northern denunciation.—Example of the Saviour. . . . . . P. 116

CHAPTER IV.

TO THE UNION.

I. What can be done? Subject of vast magnitude—radical difference of opinion.

II. Three modes of settling the question stated.

III. Faint hope that either side will abandon its position—ultra slaveholders—violence of southern excitement a favourable omen —no prospect of the North becoming in favour of slavery—reasons—will not use force against it.

IV. Dissolution of the Union considered—its probable consequences and result.

V. Third mode of settling the question—by compromise and concession—why it may be hoped for—desirable that southern men should express their views—prevented by abolition movements.

VI. Colonization recommended—abolitionists opposed—mistaken philanthropy—colonization emancipation must become a national question. South will reject every other mode—urged from motives of regard for the welfare of the coloured race—negroes cannot rise to equality with the whites—proved in the free states--in Philadelphia--slaves to remain in the country as hired servants considered--South will oppose it, and why--no encouragement from the example of the North. British emancipation referred to—final consequences not known.

VII. Why the coloured man should go to Africa--climate considered—comparisons invited--America owes it to Africa to send back her children. God intends it by our prosperity—government must do it—influences of colonization on Africa. Question of expense alluded to—money lost in Florida war.

VIII. Some slave states have begun the work—reasons for government interference—partizan politics, the curse of our country—the only hope of benevolence in the future. . P. 161

Conclusion . . . . P. 205

INTRODUCTION.

THE story of Washington and the Declaration of Independence are the first lessons treasured up in the memory by American youth; and one of the first subjects on which the reasoning powers are exerted, is an attempt to reconcile slavery with the declaration that all men " are created free and equal," and " entitled to life, liberty, and the pursuit of happiness." The youth of ingenuous disposition, educated in the free states, in reflecting upon this subject, early obtains a deep impression of the fallibility and inconsistency of human character.

First, all men are free and equal;—secondly, some of the men most distinguished in American history were slaveholders, that is, bought and sold their fellow-men like cattle;—thirdly, among these distinguished men, some (as the author of the Declaration of Independence) condemned slavery in the strongest terms of language while they lived, and others, (as General Washington,) in their final acts, cancelled the obligation of the slave, and gave him freedom.

These reflections greatly puzzled the writer of

the following pages in his boyhood, and induced a spirit of inquiry on the subject of American slavery, which has increased with maturer age. In common with the youth of the free states, he early imbibed a strong prejudice against slavery, as being incompatible with the freedom of our government: although this prejudice was subsequently somewhat softened, by reflecting, that some of the men whom Americans are taught from their childhood to venerate as great and good, were slaveholders; and also, by the consideration that the government, in all its acts and subordinate departments, has, (until very recently at least,) recognised the lawfulness of slavery. There are multitudes, doubtless, at the North, who will at once comprehend the embarrassment of the writer at this period, by their own experience;—fully convinced of the *wrong* of slavery as an *abstract* question, and yet not feeling authorized to openly denounce it, under the circumstances in which it is tolerated in our country: and it was not until the writer had mingled with slavery, and observed its practical operation and bearing upon the community, with a circumspection prompted by the curiosity and unsatisfied inquiries of twenty years' residence in the free sates, that he was enabled to form an opinion of its merits, as it exists in the United States—and also to see the reason why *great men* had been engaged in it, and why the people of the South so tenaciously adhered to the practice. The result of these observations is given in the following pages; and the writer feels an anxious interest in the diffusion of information on this subject at this time, for two reasons: 1st. A crisis is approaching. Every man of common observation must be aware of the fact, that this subject—the moral and political influence of slavery—has been increasing in public interest for the last few years; and there are evidently causes at work, which will continue to increase this interest, until public opinion shall be centred upon it with a force, which can neither be evaded nor repulsed. The rancor of a most bitter political strife has for a time withdrawn public attention from it, but the elements are yet in a state of commotion, and only wait a favourable opportunity to burst forth and overspread the whole horizon. And no honest man can, in view of our national interests, wish the settlement of this great question delayed. If slavery is that grievous, heaven-daring oppression, which some of its opposers are clamorous in denouncing, it should be speedily abolished; if it can be shown that the practice is consistent with republicanism and Christianity, the slaveholder should be relieved of that load of obloquy which many now heap upon him, and be permitted to hold his possession in peace.

I call the attention of southern men to this point. Free discussion is the only method of eliciting light, and establishing correct principles in this land of liberty. We have here no absolute monarch to think, and speak, and act for the people " by the grace of God." Free discussion is not only the prerogative but the genius of our people. It is the great manufactory of public opinion, which is the supreme law of the land. Every question, whether of village or national notoriety, must be submitted to it, and decided by it. It is as impossible to prevent this as to stop water from running down a declivity; and the attempt to arrest the progress of discussion on this great subject, if persisted in, must lead to the most disastrous results. A practice that will not bear investigation is always liable to suspicion. If the South are determined to resist every attempt to discuss and investigate the merits of slavery, it will not only increase the prejudice of its opposers, but the consequence will be to produce rival orders of public opinion at the North and South, diametrically opposed to each other, and tending to cherish sectional and jarring interests.

Without a free interchange of sentiment, there cannot be such an enlightened understanding of the subject as will lead to a righteous decision by this people. Even now there are many anxious minds labouring under an impression that slaveholders are unwilling to bring the question of slavery to a free and full discussion of its merits; and this impression is strengthened by the acts of the national legislature. At both the sessions of the twenty-fifth Congress, the House of Representatives voted (after much animated and excited debate) to reject all petitions, and to allow no discussion on the subject of slavery. This act is to be regretted. Its policy is more than questionable: it is unwise. 'It is like checking a current in its natural channel: the accumulated waters may be arrested for a time, but when the barrier gives way—as it surely must—the torrent will sweep every thing in its course. The calm which seems to acquiesce in this act, is no evidence of its approval. The fires are becoming more intense in the pent-up volcano. On a subject not involving the safety of the dearest interests of the community, a reflecting people will yield an unwilling assent to the decision of a large majority, and submit to the rejection of their petitions, constitutionally expressed and offered; until the manifest justice of their cause, and the exertions of its friends, have removed the opposition to their wishes. This mode of rejecting petitions is manifestly unjust—contrary to the spirit and letter of the constitution—and can only be defended on the ground that extreme exigences warrant the setting aside of established constitutional provisions. The slaveholder pleads that the reckless violence of the abolitionists has produced this result, and no doubt this is true; but whether the ultimate decision of the country will sustain the act, and thereby declare that the exigence required the sacrifice, time only can determine. It cannot be questioned that one effect of this act will be, a stronger conviction among the people of the North, that the South are inclined to shut up every avenue to the investigation of slavery. And the final consequences of such a conviction at the North, or such a determination at the South none can foresee, but all must dread.

2d. The object of the writer is to diffuse information on the subject among the popular ranks of his countrymen.

Many books have been already written on both sides of the question; but they have generally been elaborate treatises; on one side condemning slavery on the abstract principles of moral right, or on the other defending the practice, from the usages of mankind in all ages; or by denying and controverting the opinions of their opponents. Such works are but little suited to the popular taste, and produce but little practical effect upon the body of society. The great mass of the people, the owners and cultivators of the soil, and the artizans—men who acquire a proud independence by honest and persevering toil—who are seldom concerned in tumults or mobbish excesses,—and to whom demagogues and enthusiasts generally preach in vain—a class of men to stand by the laws in the hour of peril, and which holds in check that spirit of insubordination, which seems eager to destroy—these are the men, who are to pronounce sentence upon this momentous subject; and the sentence they pronounce they will carry into execution. But they will not decide this question, however enthusiasm may invoke, or uncurbed passion may menace, until they have had opportunity to ascertain facts, to hear evidence, and weigh the subject in all its bearings. They constitute the supreme court of the country, from whose decision there is no appeal. These men have little knowledge of Latin, or the logic of the schools, and little time to study the elaborate productions of doctors of law or metaphysics. With them a well-attested fact is of more value than a cart load of suppositions; and their assent is given to theory, when it is reduced to practice. They require no other wisdom than that plain sense with which God has endowed them—and which their observation and industry keep in constant exercise and improvement—to decide upon the most important subjects of national interest when fairly brought to their comprehension.

To this class of his fellow-countrymen, both North and South, the writer addresses these pages, without reference to politics, party, sect, or section. They have an unspeakable interest in this question; for it needs not the spirit of prophecy to foretell, that unless it be amicably settled, a crisis is approaching, which will involve the whole country, and come home to every man's bosom, from Maine to the Sabine. Already the agitation is begun, and a spirit is awakened which cannot be put to rest, till a final verdict is rendered by the people. Notwithstanding the magnitude of the subject, it is becoming one of absorbing interest, and every man in the nation must look it in the face.

To prepare the public to act understandingly, it is important that information should be diffused. Already, from ignorance of each other's circumstances, sectional animosity is gaining ground; and it will require all the wisdom which fallible men can gain from moral obligation and experience, to arrest the current of sectional prejudice, and decide the question in the spirit of equity, and with reference to the great interests at stake. That the great mass of the people are ignorant of each other's situation, and sectional and domestic customs, and therefore greatly liable to err in judging of them, the writer is abundantly satisfied from his own experience and views, before and after witnessing the operation of slavery. Should he be instrumental in directing this class of men to a sober and righteous decision on this momentous subject, his object will be attained. He has no selfish motives to favor. His own individual suggestions are alone responsible for this work. He has consulted no man, and but few books. He has no interests at stake, which will be involved by the decision of this question, any farther than as a single member of the community. The subject has been one of engrossing interest to him ever since he came to years of manhood, and he has watched the progress and development of public sentiment with great solicitude. His humble efforts are intended to direct it, in its inquiries, to a sober and thorough investigation; to a just, and, if possible, an amicable settlement of the momentous controversy.

CHAPTER I.

TO NORTHERN ABOLITIONISTS.

I. Why first appeal to Abolitionists—result of their measures doubtful.—Writer, once an abolitionist—how cured.
II. Ultraism of the present day—in theology—and benevolence.
III. Writer's views of slavery—caused by man's depravity—no remedy but Christianity—moral influence of our national prosperity.—Coronation of England's queen—Dr. Franklin.
IV. Circumstances in which slavery may be a blessing—theory and practice of abolitionists inconsistent—reference to St. Paul—objections to holding slaves.
V. Action and measures of abolitionists, why wrong—abolition periodicals—Mr. Garrison—editor in New York—should be judged charitably.
VI. Slaveholders' ideas of abolitionists—why—many slave-owners anxious to get rid of slavery—what abolitionists ought to have done—arguments not admitted—abolitionists seriously questioned.
VII. Abolition in District of Columbia opposed—why?

" One great principle which we should lay down as immovably true, is, that if a good work cannot be carried on by the calm, self-controlled, benevolent spirit of Christianity, then the time for doing it has not come." CHANNING.

I. As you had the honour or dishonour to begin the modern agitation of that great question, which has produced so much excitement in the country—the immediate abolition of slavery—it seems very proper, in taking a survey of the subject, and showing the bearing it has upon the various sections of the country, and classes of the community, to make the first appeal to you. You have declared a war of extermination against slavery, and persisted in your plans for accomplishing its overthrow, with an ardour worthy of good men in a good cause. Whether your efforts will result in the weal or wo of your country is very problematical. The principal reason to hope for the former, is, that wiser and discreeter men may arise, to wield the elements which your zeal has put in commotion. Great occasions give being and impulse to great energies, but the pioneers of a grand enterprise are seldom the men to guide it to a successful issue. In our own history, the prudence and deliberation of Franklin and Washington directed the storm which the enthusiasm and ardour of the Adamses and Henrys kindled. Without such an interference to check your headlong impetuousness, there is little hope of the future. If your past action in word and deed is to be the measure of your future progress and effort, then the patriot can only rest his hopes upon anticipations of what may be in the dispensations of Infinite Wisdom and Goodness, beyond the vision of erring and short-sighted mortals.

As one who claims an interest in the welfare of his country, not exceeded by your own—one who possesses the same freedom of opinion, and right of discussion;—as one having the same stake in the issue, and accountable to the same tribunals here and hereafter—I take the liberty to make such remarks upon your principles and measures, and offer such views respecting their ultimate tendency, as reflection and experience have suggested. In doing this, I shall use great plainness of speech; thus, in one respect at least, following your own example. But be assured, I have no sinister designs to accomplish; no feelings of enmity to gratify; and God forbid that I should cast any stumblingblock in the way, to impede the progress of truth, justice, and benevolence.

I was once a decided abolitionist in feeling—one of the "straitest sect." Looking on that side exclusively, as most of you do,—absorbed in the contemplation of the injustice and horrors of slavery, but at the same ignorant of the system—I felt almost strong enough, in view of the abstract question of right or wrong, to go forth, single-handed, to silence every opposer, and break the fetters from every slave in Christendom. A greater work than Clarkson was twenty years in accomplishing, I could have performed in about as many weeks. Such is the ardour of an ingenuous disposition in support of an exclusive idea, and just such is the great body of your members. They have read some abolition papers; heard perhaps some anti-slavery lectures, and become inflamed with a more than patriotic ardour, in defence of the great doctrine of human rights. Their arguments are very summary and conclusive. *Slavery is wrong; therefore every slaveholder ought to give his slaves instant freedom!* If his next neighbour does not immediately admit the conclusiveness of his reasoning, the abolitionist marvels at his hardness of heart, or obtuseness of intellect : if the slaveholder should plead for time to consider the subject in view of the circumstances in which he is placed, I fear the spirit of modern abolition would equal the zeal of the disciples, in wishing, on a certain occasion, to call down fire from heaven.

The writer was led to serious reflection, and ultimately cured of his abolition enthusiasm, long before he ever saw a slave, by attending the anniversaries of the Anti-slavery and Colonization Societies in New York, four or five years ago. At the meeting of the former, there was considerable exultation manifested, that the latter was labouring under great pecuniary embarrassment—one of the speakers stating to the assembly, " We have met here to sound the death-knell of colonization." At the meeting of the Colonization Society the day following, some wit was displayed, and no little mirth excited among a very reverend auditory, by alluding to the ocular proof present, that colonization was neither *dead* nor *buried*.

As a spectator the writer could not witness but with painful feelings the malevolence of disposition manifested by men claiming to be benevolent; nor could he but regret, that these two societies, having the same ultimate object in view—the improvement of the coloured race—should indulge in a bitterness of invective, not allowable even in the fiercest sectarian polemics. " Surely there is field enough for both to labour without interfering with each other; and the narrow views which engender strife and contention between them, can only be equalled by that profound charity of ignorant religionists, which will not permit an opponent to be in the way to heaven, unless he follows in the dim ray of its own little rushlight."

The scenes above mentioned gave the writer unfavourable impressions respecting the *motives* of abolitionists: since that, he has seen something of slavery in its practical appearance, and is still more unfavourably impressed with regard to their *measures*. But even these are to be judged with great allowances, except so far as they exert a practical influence injurious to society, in view of the spirit of the age.

II. Ultraism is the order of things at the present day. Every thing runs into excess. " A sober man, who can find !" The modern improvements in the arts, and the discoveries in philosophy and science, have given a kind of intoxicating impulse to men's minds; and nothing short of the velocity of steam power is sufficient to fill their enlarged capacities. Excited action is the natural result of extravagant speculation; and men, not satisfied with pitying the benighted state and groping ignorance of their fathers, seem determined to make them appear more diminutive by powerful contrast. The aged patriarch who jogs along the road in an ancient vehicle, as his fathers did before him, is rudely jostled by his flying grandchildren, who measure his wisdom and judgment by the motion of his wheels.

Theology has partaken of this spirit in a remarkable degree. The old land-marks are broken down or neglected, and new avenues are laid out to Bunyan's " celestial city." Newlight reformers have discovered that their plodding forefathers entirely erred, in explaining the text of that old guide book the Bible; and the narrow, up-hill path therein delineated has, in the plastic hands of different reformers, been smoothed and Mc Adamized; or made wide enough for all to travel together. The great change to be effected in man, may be generally produced by joining "our side;" that is the only patent orthodoxy. The attentive observer can almost hear the very language of worldly rivalry, from these modern sectarians—" this way, sir, safest and cheapest line, through by daylight."

Benevolence has also caught the same spirit, and shows a determination to make amends for the sluggish apathy of all former generations. Let me not be understood as being opposed to benevolent enterprize. Among the almost innumerable societies for improving the condition of the human family, no doubt the most of them are exerting a happy influence. There can be no danger of circulating too many Bibles, or religious tracts, or Sunday-school books; nor of employing too many devoted missionaries. There is vice, and crime, and misery enough in the world, to employ all the hands, and hearts, and means, which Christian charity can call into action. But there is a great amount of zeal on this subject which is not according to knowledge. Among the innumerable demands made on the public for its aid in sustaining charitable and benevolent operations, there is difficulty in deciding upon the most worthy objects. The incessant call for giving, has influenced many to withhold altogether. And there is evidently a spirit of competition excited among some societies for public favour, and a jealousy of each others success. But on this subject, as almost every other, enthusiasm has far outstripped sober judgment. Men's minds have become so absorbed in the contemplation of existing evils, that they seem incapable of adopting the best mode of removing them.

This I believe is true in regard to the subject of slavery. Among the great objects of modern benevolence, the slave receives, at the present moment, an unusual share of commiseration. The subject is indeed one of unspeakable interest, and worthy the attention of every philanthropist; but its very magnitude should teach us to approach it with caution. Instead of this, a numerous class appear bent upon deciding it in a summary manner. The abolitionists have no idea of allowing any circumstances to affect their belief or to modify their measures. They have seized hold of this, with an exclusiveness of purpose, as though it were the only sin of the age, and, in their zeal for its removal, have leaped over every consideration affecting the situation of those most deeply interested, both masters and slaves: and their loud, and unceasing cry is, *repent, repent.* Surely the eyes which see such grievous beams in others, should be clear of motes; and the hearts which condemn such hardness should be full of Christian charity and meekness. But I fear the abolitionists are not so guiltless of all sin, as to be authorized to throw the first stone at slaveholders.

III. In making this brief appeal, I shall state

First, My own views with regard to slavery; and,

Secondly, My views respecting the plans and measures of abolitionists, and their ultimate tendency.

Abstractly considered, slavery has been proved to be a grievous wrong. It would require very little reasoning to convince a free man of common intelligence and common uprightness that he possessed inherent rights and faculties, of which he could not be justly deprived, except by the Creator who bestowed them. Nor would it be difficult to prove to him, that his fellow-men, by whom he is surrounded, are entitled to the same privileges as himself, being given by the same Author. The equality of men in essential things, in likeness of physical organization, in the attributes of body and mind, is too evident to admit a doubt that God intended each to be free and happy; responsible only to Him for the possession and exercise of those endowments and faculties which he alone could give or take away.

Were these great principles, which lie at the very foundation of our *theory* of government, acted upon by the human family, there would be no crime, no misery, no tyranny, no slavery in the world, and a community, whether large or small, will be individually and socially happy, and approximate towards perfection, just in proportion to its adoption and practice of these principles. But alas! we are speaking of principles which have had but a very limited influence among men since the garden of Eden was deserted; and which will never prevail in the world, till God regenerates our race.

It will not probably be heresy in the view of abolitionists to declare a belief in that ancient doctrine, the fall of man from his original rectitude, that event which

"Brought death into the world and all our wo."

From that period to the present, man, having lost the moral image of his Maker, has followed the devices of his own heart; what these are, the Bible will inform us: and the history of five thousand years will attest the truth of the record. Without holy affections, without innocence, mankind prefer the pleasures of sense to moral obedience. And as God has so ordered, that his laws cannot be broken with impunity, either in the moral or physical world, just so far as men have trampled upon the authority of God, have they become obnoxious to the penalty of transgression. This penalty is exacted in the moral world—in the guilty conscience, the shame of discovery, the fear of punishment and of future retribution. In the physical, it is seen in the shape of every evil that "flesh is heir to." Tyranny and oppression, beastly vice, haggard poverty, sickness and death, are its unerring results. God never made a man to be a slave, neither did he ever make one to be sick, or poor, or unhappy. But sickness and poverty are the certain consequences of the transgression of the immutable laws of Providence; nor does slavery constitute an exception. There can be no doubt that the regular action of the functions of the human system will always preserve health: it is only their obstruction by intemperance and excess which produces disease; and this obstruction when complete must necessarily end in the premature dissolution of the body. So in civil communities, did each regard the great laws of individual and equal rights, joined with the evident acquirements of duty, to be industrious and temperate, peace and happiness would universally follow. But it is this disregard of the order of Providence which obstructs healthy action in society, just as in the human system. Men are very sagacious to discover, and very prompt to assist their own inherent rights and privileges, but the equal rights of others are not included in their process of reasoning.

And the same cause which makes the monarch

an oppressor, makes his servant a brute. Both have cast off their obligations, and each is pursuing his self-gratification in the course most agreeable to his condition. Perhaps in the next generation their situations may be reversed: the son of the tyrant may be a groveling beast; the other an oppressive despot. But from the circumstances of men in most countries, comparatively few can be lords or tyrants. Wealth, and talent, and hereditary privilege generally combine to hold the reins of power, but the avenues to sensual gratification are open to all. Hence the mass of men, by indulging their propensities for such gratifications as are within their reach, have been in every age debased and vicious. The gradations are many, but the tendency is always downward; and vast numbers in every community have ever been at the bottom of the scale. They have yielded every sentiment of honour and humanity to the inexorable demands of a brutalizing lust; have suffered the fire of heaven to be extinguished in their bosoms, or given themselves over, self-bound, to be beasts of burden. In elevating the scale of human character from cannibalism to civilization and Christianity, there is a stronger assertion of national right and individual thought; but even at the highest point yet attained, the structure of society is like the feet of the image in Nebuchadnezzar's vision, part of iron and part of clay.

In this highly favoured country—if a digression from the subject may be allowed—the community appear to be intoxicated with the idea that the golden age is returning; when liberty and equal rights, emanating from this union as a centre, will overspread the world. I invoke the blessing of Heaven, that this feeling, so extensively pervading the public mind, may not prove to be a mere fit of intoxication, and nothing more nor worse. But let us not be deceived. I fear we are anticipating the most important effects, from very inadequate causes—looking for good fruit from an evil tree. As a nation, although but just emerged from childhood, we have made some progress in the arts, some in science, much in improvements of practical utility; and are perhaps in advance of all others in the freedom of our constitution. But we are as yet scarcely on the threshold of civil liberty. Unless we enter far enough to see the beauty and glory of the inner temple, our worship will be confined merely, as it has been in all ages, to the dazzling exterior. There is a charm which captivates, in the sound of liberty; but unless it has its seat in the heart of pure moral affections, its exercise cannot be depended on for guiding its possessor aright, or for exerting a salutary influence upon others.

Nothing but the spirit of Christianity can elevate us as a people. No man but a Christian can be a true republican, in the highest and best sense of the term. Of freedom of opinion and action we have enough, more perhaps than the mass of men (liable as they are to be swayed by corrupt and unprincipled partizans) know how to exercise to advantage; and unless our moral improvement advances in the front rank of our social progress, the liberty to do wrong will eventually overcome the disposition to do right. Could the arts have regenerated the world, it would not be in so deplorable a condition; for it is a question even now, whether Egypt, three thousand years ago, was not our superior. Could literature have done it, then the Augustan Age had stayed that long night of darkness which overspread twelve centuries of our era. And of science, it will not be too much to say, that it has been always harnessed to the car of ambition, and its highest attainments oftener exerted for the destruction than the welfare of man.

Intelligence without piety is like the giant in the fable, strong and blind, more likely to do evil than good. An intellect that could measure the universe, would not promote the best interests of man, without being guided by a sense of moral obligation. Political economists and philosophers, reasoning *à priori*, have concluded that there is necessarily a period of advancement, of elevation, and decline in national affairs. Because Egypt, and Assyria, and Rome, rose, and reigned, and declined, therefore all nations must. Such a doctrine is a libel on the divine character; a stretch of assumption which even infidelity has hardly dared to make. It is mere fatalism—an adoption of one of the grossest sentiments of heathen mythology, that the fates are above the gods themselves. Such a doctrine teaches but one thing conclusively; and that, some of its advocates would abhor, viz., the entire depravity of man. That communities and nations have not continued to rise and flourish, the history of the past is a melancholy proof: but to say they *cannot*, is to question the sincerity, authority, and power of Jehovah, in his warnings, exhortations, and promises to the Israelites in the Mosaic record.

In pursuing these reflections a little further, suffer me to inquire, what is the ultimate object of all our toil? what the glittering prize, which enlarges our organs of vision? What the great idol on whose altar the whole community is mad? Is it any thing higher than lofty conceptions of individual and national aggrandizement? Whence is the loud boast of our commerce, our manufactures, our internal resources, our rail-roads and canals? Is it any thing more than the flattering belief that these will elevate us in power and grandeur above the nations? Without suitable acknowledgments of the Divine sovereignty, and a heartfelt conviction of our dependence, and obligations to Him, as our constant benefactor; the blessings which are poured into our lap without measure, will only enlarge our ability, and increase our dispositions to do evil. We have the Bible in proof, " The *love* of money is the root of all evil." Was there ever a people whose entire energies were so devotedly consecrated to the acquisition of gain, as ours? And there is greater cause for apprehension in the fact, that religion has, to a great extent, caught the spirit, and appears ambitious to follow the maxims, and keep up with the improvements of the world. Her temples are crowded—her votaries innumerable; for the profession is in honor. Who are indeed striving for "a crown of glory that fadeth not away" will only be known, when the Son of God shall come to claim his jewels. Heaven will not lack inhabitants, if it be as easy to join the church triumphant as to get into the church (miscalled) militant.

Still, there is hope of our country, in the diffusion of the means of light—in the spread of the Bible—in the sacrifices for missions—in the extension of Sunday-schools, and more in that unobtrusive piety, which seeks out the objects of its benevolence among the wretched, and mingles its prayers and tears with the neglected outcast, unknown to the world; leaving its reward to "the resurrection of the just." I would rather rest the welfare and safety of my country, on the intercessions of one such soul, than on the valor of the mightiest captain. Ten such souls would have saved Sodom. A nation of such would convert the world.

It was a beautiful emblem of the ancient Greeks in lighting their altar fires from the sun. The offering of common fire was unworthy the deity they invoked. They undoubtedly borrowed the idea from the Israelites, whose altars were sometimes kindled by fire miraculously descended: but although they had lost the knowledge of the true

God, they kept up the allusion in drawing fire from the principal object of his visible creation. In proportion to the number of hearts, which are daily kindled with fire from heaven, will our country obtain the protection and blessing of Infinite benevolence.

I will close this digression, by referring to a fact of recent occurrence, which has been a subject of serious reflection, from its contrast with parallel scenes in our own country. I allude to the late crowning of the Queen of England. In view of the wealth and power of the British empire, the splendor and talent of the embassies which came to do it honour, it was perhaps the grandest and most magnificent pageant which the world ever witnessed. But the fact to which the attention of the reader is directed, is the religious, yea, devotional spirit of the august ceremonies. The high priest of all England appears to have been the second personage in the scale of attractions on that solemn occasion. The sacred anthems, the services of the church, the offerings, the presence of the Bible, and the distinct acknowledgment of its Author, as the source whence " kings reign and princes decree justice," presented a spectacle worthy of a Christian nation, and which cannot but have a happy influence upon its morals and institutions. Would that our republican legislators might so far overcome their patriotic horror of the union of church and state, as at least in their public ceremonies of national interest to acknowledge the sovereignty and beneficence of the Supreme Governor of the universe, and give pious hearts in their vast assemblies an opportunity and an impulse to invoke the blessings of God upon their public servants and their own beloved country.

There is indeed one event in our own history, which will be remembered as an instance of the moral sublime, and one on which a good man cannot reflect without the keenest emotion. It was when Franklin arose in the Congress which adopted our constitution, and acknowledged there was a God who ruled in the affairs of men, and proposed that prayers be daily offered, for His wisdom and guidance through the angry and stormy strife which impeded all their deliberations. I am not aware that Franklin was a professor of religion; but this act of his will increase the veneration for his character and services among the good and wise of his countrymen in all generations.

IV. To return from this digression to the question of slavery.

If the view we have taken of the moral state of man be correct—if the tendency of human nature, when left to itself, is headlong downward—then slavery, by arresting the progress of man in his brutalizing course, may prove a blessing. For this reason, God has permitted slavery, probably, to avoid a greater evil. On this principle can I account for the plain declarations of scripture in the

Old Testament. I know not how a proposition can be expressed more plainly in words, than the permission given the Israelites to hold slaves. Lev. xxv. 44--46. This is more than mere permission, it is authority; and the reason for it is plain, on the principle I have assumed. Of the heathen round about them, the Israelites might buy servants to serve them for ever. The moral and physical condition of such persons would be greatly improved as slaves to the Israelites; in comparison with their lot as heathen, sunk in the grossest idolatry and brutality.

And on this principle, I understand the curse pronounced upon Ham, Gen. ix. 25--27; not that it was for ever absolute and irreversible; but that Ham was so debased and prone to vice—his very affections were so given up to the greedy pursuit of sinful indulgence—that servitude to his brethren would be the means of restraining him and his posterity from the lowest depth of wretchedness.

And nowhere in the Bible is the possession of slaves prohibited. I know it is contended, that the great law of loving our neighbour as ourself utterly condemns it. There can be no doubt among good men, that when the principles of this law prevail in the world, there will be no slavery. But I cannot find any example or authority in sacred history, for agitating its overthrow; except by such a diffusion of the light of the Gospel, as shall naturally produce its extinction. It is evidently left by the

Saviour and apostles as an evil appertaining to the present state of man, to be overthrown by the gradual adoption of the principles of Christianity.

In illustration of this it may be remarked, that there was probably never a people in a state of greater moral delinquency, than the Jews in the time of our Saviour. Slavery among them, and among their masters the Romans, was a cup of unmingled bitterness. The slaves of that period drank it to the dregs. And yet Jesus Christ did not preach insurrection or insubordination to the slave, nor condemn the owner for possessing them. It was no part of his mission to change the institutions of society by a miracle. He did not interfere with established usages and customs. He admitted the order of society as he found it. "Render unto Cesar the things that are Cesars." The great principles of morals he inculcated, when adopted by an individual, will teach him the love of God and man; when adopted by a community, will overthrow every evil which that community has cherished or practised. It was his object to make the tree good; not by a miracle to produce good fruit from an evil tree. Of what advantage would it have been to mankind, had he freed the slaves, without giving them and their masters new motives of action? On this point it appears to me, the abolitionists greatly err, in pressing the immediate and unconditional emancipation of the slaves in our country, without considering the consequences which would result to masters and servants from such an act.*

Again, this rule of doing to others what we would have them do to us, was never taken in its broadest literal signification. Such a construction is not sustained by the Bible, nor the institutions of the wisest men. In the present moral state of the world, it would lead at once to the dissolution of society. Its legitimate effect would be an agrarian division of property, and another subdivision, as soon as the improvident and vicious had wasted their dividend. The abolitionists will contend that by this rule the master ought to treat his slaves as his children. But who ever did it? who ever required it? They will not certainly object to be judged by their works. Are *their* servants on an equality with *their* children? Do they eat, and drink, and sleep with them, as with their children—send them to the same schools—occupy the same seats in the church—use the same means to train them up? Do they alternately send their daughters into the kitchen, and bring their maid servants into the parlour to acquire polite accomplishments? " Consistency *is* a jewel." Have they first cast the motes out of their own eyes? Their practice in the circumstances above mentioned is sufficient proof that they do not regard the exhortation of the apostle, " masters, give to your servants that which is just and equal," as a command to make

---

* The reader is referred to the writer's views on this subject more fully in another part of this work,—Appeal to the Free States.

them equals. If the inspired writer had intended to make them free by this injunction, he would not have used the term *servants*, which implies subjection.

Subordination and gradation prevail throughout the world,—and they will forever. I speak it with reverence, they prevail in heaven. The creation of different orders of intelligence requires it: and this is perfectly consistent with the moral government of God. In a state of unmingled joy and happiness, every being will enjoy the blessing to the extent of his capacity, but the capacities of all will not be equal.

Again, to refer to the doctrines and example of the New Testament on this subject, I can but wish our modern abolitionists would drink in more of the spirit, and copy more the example of St. Paul. We read that on one occasion, "his spirit was stirred within him when he saw the city wholly given to idolatry." That city was as full of slavery as of idolatry; but we do not read of any denunciations against it in the language and spirit of modern abolitionism. He even did not rail and scoff at their idolatry. Did Paul in his epistles teach servants that insubordination, or obedience, was well-pleasing unto God? Did he *exhort* masters to treat their slaves in view of an accountability hereafter, and in the fear of God? or did he denounce them as deserving of utter wrath for the mere act? Did he teach submission or rebellion to the laws?—even of tyrants. Did he bring railing accusations against those who opposed him?—or was he content to say "the Lord reward him according to his works?" Did he assist and secrete runaway slaves?—or return such to their Christian masters? What was his course in the vineyard of his Lord, in the midst of a most ungodly generation—but one of meekness, forbearance, patience, prayers, and tears! These are evidences, known and read of all men, of the spirit and power of Christianity, for they are qualities and virtues which do not flourish in the hearts, nor show themselves in the practices of the world.

On the principles heretofore mentioned, I hold the doctrine of slavery. I believe the sin to be in the *abuse*, rather than the *use* of slaves. I cannot think of any circumstances in which I would purchase a slave—except to manumit him; but have no hesitation in declaring my conviction, that should slaves fall into my hands by marriage, inheritance, or otherwise, I *might possess* them, and so discharge my duty towards them, as to avoid condemnation of heaven. On this point, I have no doubt; but may God spare me the trial. It is a fearful responsibility to have one's temporal and eternal destiny put into his own hands: who, then, is sufficient to incur that of many others in addition to his own? I should fear the result, when my principles and self-interest were at strife, over a rational, immortal being like myself, and his welfare was the stake. His moral accountability, his life and health, his riches and poverty, his virtue and vice, his ignorance and knowledge, would be so much under my control, that on my head must rest a fearful obligation.

But there is another objection which, as an individual, I should plead against holding slaves; and which, although of an entirely different character from the one just mentioned, would be conclusive, viz., their comparative worthlessness as laborers. Except in a country where Divine Providence has poured out its bounty upon the soil with an unsparing hand, they are not profitable. On a sterile or exhausted soil they are a moth, scarcely producing their living. If this fact is an argument against slavery, so be it: it is no part of my design to shield it from fair and close investigation.

Before leaving this part of the subject I wish to anticipate a question, which many readers may wish to propose,—" Admitting the correctness of your views respecting slavery, would it not be more consistent with our professions, as a moral, benevolent people, to endeavour to teach and elevate the poor and degraded, rather than by consigning them to bondage, merely coerce them into a state of negative goodness?" Certainly. No man who has the most distant pretension to Christian character, can hesitate to decide this point. But the question, in this form, does not apply to our subject. We are not to consider the propriety, expediency, or sinfulness of adopting certain *measures;* but the influence of measures which have been adopted, and incorporated into society for generations. The difference is as great, I apprehend, as between deciding whether a certain regimen if adopted, will injure a man's health; and the best method of counteracting the effects of that regimen upon the system, after it has been practised for years, and found to be pernicious.

V. I purpose to make some remarks upon the plans and measures of abolitionists.

And, first, it appears almost evident, that a conviction must force itself upon the minds of sober reflecting men, who have taken an interest in this controversy, that the abolitionists have not followed the Christian rule laid down by the Saviour, Matt. xviii. 15, nor the golden rule, of doing as they would have others do to them. On the abstract question of right and wrong, they commenced a most violent attack upon slaveholders indiscriminately; denouncing them all as guilty of a most horrible, unnatural crime; and with an assurance unbecoming fallible men, anticipating the extreme judgments of Heaven. And then, for accomplishing its overthrow, they took a step, for the *wisdom* of which the history of the world can not furnish a parallel. That step was, the sending of these bitter, indiscriminate denunciations all over the South, hurling their direful anathemas in the face of a community, which neither acknowledged their right to judge, nor the correctness of their assumptions.

2d. As an appendage to these denunciations, they held up slavery as a monster of cruelty, and impurity, and oppression; virtually saying to every slaveholder who received one of these inflammatory papers, "thou art the man." Can it be wondered at, if the whole South was instantly in a blaze. For my own part, I am only surprised, that the utterance of southern feeling and indignation was not more outrageous. The unanimity of the South, in repelling these attacks, and throwing back these denunciations is without a parallel. Not only the slaveholder from *principle*, but the thousands who were anxiously looking for some way to abolish it, all united in resisting this wanton attack. Even now, in the national and state legislatures, every question is viewed by southern men with regard to the bearing it has upon immediate abolition.

In another respect the action of abolitionists has been contrary to every principle of justice, rectitude, and fairness. As a body they know comparatively nothing of practical slavery, and yet they continually denounce it for its cruelty. They have seized hold of individual instances of great tyranny and personal oppression, and charge the crime upon the whole community. This is manifestly unjust. By the same rule every denomination of Christians—yea, Christianity itself—might be condemned. Probably not one person in a hundred who has subscribed to abolition societies and petitions, has ever been in a slave state. Their information is derived, in a great measure, from travelers and transient residents—many of whose statements are of an exparte character, and of whom comparatively few had sufficient opportunities, or took sufficient interest in the subject, to judge it fairly or comprehensively. The inhabitants of the free states, who have never been at the South, can form no more definite ideas of the practical operation of slavery, than they can of the face of a country, from the description of a traveler. The traveler will show you a hill here, and a valley there, but of the numberless inequalities of surface, a single view will give you a correcter idea, than a hundred pages of description. So on this subject, it is impossible to form a comprehensive view of the detail of slavery, without actual inspection. The writer had conversed with, and questioned hundreds respecting it, but two days' actual observation gave him altogether a clearer view of the system of *what slavery is*, than the answers to a thousand questions.

Another measure of abolitionists, which has been the cause of much excitement, was the invitation and cordial reception given to a foreign emissary to denounce slavery, at the North. This excited feelings of great irritation at the South, as it did feelings of humiliation among the majority in the free states. It was in effect declaring that Americans were not capable of managing their own domestic concerns, without foreign interference. Had this missionary gone to the South, as the appropriate field of his labours, it would have been in character; but his moral courage could not have been of a very high order, to shoot his artillery from behind a barrier, and fear to meet his opponents face to face. The views of the writer at that period were inclined to favour abolition, but as an American he heartily rejoiced that this intermeddling philanthropist was driven from the country by the force of public sentiment, without personal injury.

Again, the resolutions introduced and carried, and the speeches delivered at abolition meetings, are frequently characterized by illiberality; full of violent and bitter denunciation against the whole South, without respect to age, sex, or character. If we are to believe some of them, the ministers of the slaveholding states are more deserving the Penitentiary than the pulpit. Such wholesale maledictions are a source of constant irritation, exciting deep feelings of prejudice and animosity at the South, and they retard the progress of true benevolence.

In connexion with this may be mentioned the abolition periodicals. I regret to say they are far, immeasurably, below that standard of Christian forbearance and moderation, which should characterize the discussion of so important a subject. They have descended from that elevation which should ever be sustained in pleading the cause of humanity and philanthropy, to wallow in the dirty waters of malevolence and abuse. A good cause never requires the aid—is never promoted by the use—of opprobrious language. " Soft words and hard arguments" is the maxim of Christianity; not feeble arguments in harsh words. It seems almost impossible for a paragraph writer on the abolition side, not to get into a passion, and to scatter firebrands on all sides of him. Not satisfied with depicting scenes of inhuman cruelty and oppression which he never witnessed, he pours vials of wormwood and gall upon a whole community.

Among these periodicals the "Liberator" deserves notice, as being the oldest; the great pioneer of anti-slavery. I never read it except as accident threw it in my way; but it will be safe to assert, that I never saw a copy, which did not contain sentences and epithets, which Christianity would blush to own. One of these papers, the only one seen for a year, now lies before me. I will copy a few sentences in proof of the statement above. The writer is speaking of some colonizationist in New Jersey. It ought to be stated, however, that this communication is not original in the Liberator, but adopted from another paper.

"One Honourable persecuting inquisitor, who has more presumption than brains, already in a certain neighbourhood, has done more mischief, and created more prejudice against the poor unoffending coloured people, and thrown more difficulties in their way, than his body hung upon pitch-forks could atone for in purgatory, in a thousand generations. Contemptible wretch! Is it not enough that coloured men are already sought out and abused by every vagabond in the land, through colonization instrumentality? will this grayheaded totterer upon the brink of the grave and of eternity, fill up the measure of his iniquity by becoming more notorious for cruelty and wickedness than Satan himself?"

I will leave this extract, with the single observation, that I have entirely mistaken the character of the people in New England, if they sustain a cause which is supported by such language, and such a temper as the above.

It is with no pleasure these references are made to the Liberator. For the writer had formed a high opinion of Mr. Garrison—tinctured no doubt with boyish enthusiasm—from an anecdote which is current in some parts of the North. It is this:—His mother consecrated him to the work of slave emancipation from childhood; instilled into his youthful bosom a horror of the practice; and charged him to prosecute its abolition, as the great purpose of his earthly being. The writer disclaims all intention of injuring any person by relating this anecdote, nor does he indorse its correctness. Even if it be true, it will not be believed that Mr. Garrison imbibed the gall and bitterness of his paper from such a source; and perhaps there are palliating circumstances in the fact, that he has been publicly denounced as an incendiary, and a reward offered for his apprehension and delivery to the South. But a man who places himself in the front rank in a great moral enterprize, must not only forego all stipulations affecting his personal destiny, but should bear himself above the petty strife and clamor of the multitude. It is *painful* to reflect, that in a man of his talents and influence, the " milk of human kindness" should so soon be dried up, or that he should ever be girded with other armour than that which becomes a Christian philanthropist.

And the abolition periodicals abound in *such* Christian sentiments. 1 will instance one more—from a reverend editor in New York:—" Truly, we believe the destiny of the most abhorred beings that ever lived on earth, will be mild compared with the reprobation that awaits the clerical defenders of American slavery." Then perdition unavoidably awaits nine tenths of the ministers of all denominations south of the Potomac and Ohio. And oh! such an aggravated doom! The writer has some clerical acquaintance in the slave states, who he had no doubt —until this malediction appeared—would be found worthy to walk the streets of the New Jerusalem; and even now he will continue to hope, reflecting with respect to these men in the spirit of a royal and a grievous sinner of old, who in the depth of his penitence said, " who can tell ?"

But the above, and similar expressions from the same paper, should be read with great allowances; for the writer can bear witness that this same reverend editor is a very serious, conscientious, estimable man, except when he is seized with these terrible ague-fits of immediate abolition. He is indeed, upon the whole, a very fair reasoner on the subject of slavery; but occasionally, after preparing a very palatable dish, even for his opponents, he will, in one of these paroxysms, dash in wormwood enough to nauseate even his friends.

The writer would suggest in the kindest manner to this reverend editor to commence a series of essays on *charity,* founded upon the thirteenth chapter of First Corinthians. By keeping the skeleton in the drawer of his editorial table, where he could seize it in a moment, and employ a half hour in filling it up, when he felt one of these wormwood fits coming on, it might greatly promote the cause of rational abolition.

There is one feature in many of the productions of abolitionists to which I would seriously call their attention, as it is evidently proof either of an unusual degree of human frailty or of superhuman knowledge. They are very much inclined to extend their denunciations beyond the limits of time, and assign their opponents to a doom more or less aggravated, it would seem, in proportion to their want of faith in, or opposition to, the scheme of immediate abolition. From the example of the Bible, it appears that the future destiny of sinners was seldom pronounced except by Him who knew what was in man—an apostle but in one instance saying—" *thou* child of the devil;" and even an angel, when disputing with an opponent, was content to say, " the Lord rebuke thee."

VI. Permit me now to state, what the abolitionists have already effected at the South.

And first, they have loaded themselves with not

only the indignation, but the deep execration of nearly a whole community. It is impossible for language to express the feelings of slaveholders on this point. Imagine a monster with the heart of a fiend and the strength of a tiger; which delighted in filling a peaceful hamlet with midnight shrieks and consternation—that monster would be an approximation to an abolitionist, in the mind of a southern slaveholder. I do not use this language as mere declamation—but only express the ideas which have been conveyed to the mind, through the medium of the eye and the ear.

And the question immediately arises; have they deserved this execration? As an individual I do not hesitate to say, they are not altogether guiltless. The reasons for this opinion have been recapitulated. It has been stated that abolitionists are not proper judges of slavery, for as a body they know nothing about it; and it is equally true, that as a body, slaveholders are not proper judges of abolitionists, and for the same reason. Just in this position the parties stand at present, ignorant of each other's characters and motives; but vindictively urgent in hurling at each other the most violent denunciations, and applying the grossest epithets of abuse which language can furnish. It is impossible to say which has the advantage in this contest, but it must be admitted that the abolitionists were the aggressors.

Secondly. The abolitionists could not have devised a plan, more effectually to close up every avenue leading to slave emancipation, than the measures which have been referred to. They have greatly increased a feeling of jealousy and suspicion towards the North; and they have rivetted the fetters of the slave, abridging the few pleasures he enjoyed, and throwing serious obstacles in the way of his redemption. I had often heard this stated as one of the results of abolition movements, but gave it little credit, believing it to be the outcry of persons interested in the perpetuation of slavery. But a very slight acquaintance with the South will place its truth beyond a doubt. Pass over the boundary between the free and slave states, at any point you please; and as you advance, ask the inhabitants their views of abolition, and the effect its measures have had in abridging the liberty of the slave. If the answers are not unanimous, as to the fact, and the cause, I will retract the statement.

In all the frontier slave states, several causes have conspired to work a change in the public mind prejudicial to slavery, for some years past. This change had operated so far in most of these states, as to produce more or less action touching the question of slavery in the state legislatures. In Virginia particularly, the subject had been freely discussed with respect to measures for prospective emancipation, and the people were watching the progress of legislation with great interest. Almost in a moment, the subject was dropped, when it was seen what course the abolitionists were pursuing;

and instead of measures for giving freedom to slaves, it was considered necessary to make additional laws for their security; and to counteract what were looked upon as incendiary movements in the free states.

Could abolitionists hear *good men* (for although it may not be credited every where, there are good men among slaveholders), I repeat, could they hear good men in Virginia deplore this, as one of the injurious results of their measures, they would ponder their doings with more deliberation. The wheels which had begun to move, and were acquiring accelerated motion by the action of public sentiment, were effectually blocked; and they could never be set in motion again until the obstacle was removed. When the whole South was assailed with denunciation, and threatened with ruin and perdition, it was to be expected that all parties and opinions should sink their private views and minor interests in the public welfare, and unite in opposing the common enemy. Thus the public agitation of the subject has been indefinitely postponed through the mistaken zeal of abolitionists.

There can be little doubt in the minds of those acquainted with the subject, that had there been no cause of reaction, public opinion would have directed legislation to provide for prospective emancipation, in more than one of the slave states, in a very few years; probably the work would have been commenced at the present moment. There is a continual outcry among a certain class of agitators, from one end of the slave states to the other, appealing to southern interests, and southern feelings, and having a direct reference to the institution of slavery. This is a bond of union indeed, and one which will not be easily dissolved; but there is a stronger bond even than this which governs men, and that is individual interest. And rest assured, that just as soon as a majority of the talent, the wealth, the free population of any state decides that slavery is injurious to the best interests of that state, it will be abandoned, notwithstanding all the influence which may be brought to oppose it. And there are powerful causes at work, tending to produce this result, in all the frontier slave states.

Were the writer to undertake a mission to the South to preach against slavery, he would, at least in tl e five most northern states, take *political economy* for his text, and engage to convert fourfold more slaveholders than could abolitionists.

But the last thing that can be done, will be *to drive* them into emancipation. Almost every thing in this world can be driven from its position, but human nature; and of this genus, perhaps the American is the most intractable species; and of the American, the southern will claim its full share of pertinacity in maintaining its opinions and defending its practices.

Had abolitionists adopted a different course, they might have effected great good—perhaps the accomplishment of their object, slave emancipation. Instead of confining their attention chiefly to the abstract question of moral right and wrong, and bitterly reproaching the advocates of slavery on their own assumption of the decision, they had deliberated and inquired as other men, and even as they do on other subjects, they would now sustain a very different attitude before the community. Had they at first made an appeal to the South openly, and not as spies—in the spirit of Christian forbearance and meekness, appealing to their hearts and consciences as responsible and accountable stewards, they would have found many persons willing to listen to all their rebukes, and ready to confer with them respecting any feasible plan for the abolition of slavery. Had they gone, not as agents of societies, but as simple individuals, and examined slavery critically, in the various aspects of its practical operation, they would have been better able to judge of its enormity, and to apply a suitable remedy. Had they preached the doctrines of the New Testament—not on the house-tops but at the fireside—they would have found multitudes ready to respond to the truth, and would have been received with courtesy and Christian hospitality.

But let them not go now, as avowed abolitionists, unless they aspire to a national notoriety. They would hardly escape the honor of martyrdom, below the thirty-fifth degree of latitude: above that line they might receive some permanent badge of southern sensibility. And yet at this day, there is no hesitation in a Virginian to converse freely, and express his views frankly respecting slavery to a guest, who gives evidence that he has no sinister design in view.

There are thousands of slaveholders who are as anxious to get rid of slavery as abolitionists are to have them—though not in all cases, *for precisely the same reason.* Perhaps the latter may take to themselves the credit of this fact, but let them not be deceived. The persons with whom the writer conversed, who most deeply regretted the existence of slavery among them, could scarcely restrain their indignation when alluding to the abolitionists for having effectually (at least for the present) put a stop to all the plans in progress for the removal of the evil. Perhaps it may not be universally known, that the law prevents masters from giving freedom to their slaves, unless they are sent out of the state; or bonds are required for their maintenance and good behaviour.

The creed of the abolitionist may be summed up in one sentence—"do right, and leave consequences to God." This reads very well, but in the view of slaveholders it is mere assumption, inasmuch as it implies that slavery is *not* right. The majority of slaveholders are conscious of no wrong in the practice. And a very little reflection, or a limited acquaintaince ith human nature, might have taught the abolitionists, that a system of so long standing, incorporated into society for ages, combining the influence of almost the entire community, would not surrender at discretion. They might have known that, however individuals of that community might be affected by the question, there were multitudes upon whom their belief would have no effect; who would spurn their anathemas, and scoff at dictation on a subject in which their own interests were immediately and vitally concerned. Foreseeing this, probably, and wishing to array all the opposition to it in one combination, they have exerted themselves in forming a system of affiliated societies in the free states; hoping, perhaps, by their exertions, and trusting to the numerical strength and intelligence of the North, to bear down slavery by the concentrated force of public opinion.

But are they sure of being *right* in this view of the subject. On this point, I would bespeak their most serious and deliberate attention. They profess to be governed by very disinterested and pure motives, appealing to the Bible for arguments in defence of their measures, and for their rectitude of motive. But supposing they should succeed in concentrating public opinion at the North against slavery: is that opinion so enlightened, that it would be controlled by the spirit of the Gospel? If not, then its concentration against slavery would only produce evil, being governed by selfish motives. I confess a decided belief, that the concentration of public opinion in the free states, (enlightened and pious as they are,) would, at present, be swayed much more strongly by political than by religious motives. There are indications that anti-slavery is becoming drawn into the vortex of politics ; if so, it will at once descend from its peculiar position, and be merged in the strife of parties; or should it become sufficiently influential to make itself the most prominent subject of party action—which it will never do, until its tone is changed—it would lead at once to decisive, perhaps, fatal measures. But as the stream cannot rise above its fountain, neither can the moral agency of a society exceed the moral aggregate of its members. If the abolitionists, by any possible event, should succeed in obtaining a majority in the state and national councils ; and should then press their measures in the same spirit they now manifest; can they depend upon the moral power of that majority to wield the elements in the storms that may arise? Have abolitionists deeply pondered the event of success in their headlong course?

VII. There is one more subject, having a most important bearing on this question, to which I wish briefly to allude, in closing this chapter. The abolitionists have become clamorous for the expurgation of the District of Columbia. Their efforts on this point are destined, I candidly believe, *to be productive of evil.* On this subject, sober reflection has made an entire revolution in my opinion.

First. The South will always resist the proposition. They will never consent to the measure (nor can they consistently) until they are ready to abolish slavery in the states. They look upon this district in the light of a frontier post adjoining an enemy's territory, the yielding of which would open an avenue for their admission into the whole country. Under these circumstances, the continual agitation of the question must be a source of exceeding irritation and apprehension. And in the zeal which the people of the North have manifested on this subject, it appears they have lost something of that reputation for staidness and deliberation for which they are wont to be characterized. I say the people of the North, for I am persuaded but a part of those signing the petitions for abolition in the District of Columbia, would agree with the abolitionists in their abuse, and their indiscriminate and unchristian denunciation of the South. Comparatively few of the petitioners on the long rolls sent to Congress ever deliberately canvassed the subject, or seriously reflected upon the consequences of *the success of their petition.* They have perhaps heard an anti-slavery lecture, and the petition is passed round at the close, while the thermometer of public feeling is above blood-heat, under the influence of the eloquent lecture; or some busy-body with a long tongue in a small head goes through the neighbourhood with the instrument of abolition in his hand, and lectures by families. His eloquence magnetises wherever it falls, and the fever becomes contagious. The deacon signs it because the minister did; the farmer because the squire did; and all their hirelings, to be in good company. Is it not so?"

Secondly. Although it is admitted that Congress

has unlimited power in the district, yet it may be questioned, whether an act to abolish slavery there would be in all respects an act of good faith. That part of the district in which the city of Washington is situated was formerly an integral part of the state of Maryland. Would she have resigned her jurisdiction over this territory, had she known that Congress would have abolished slavery in it? And if not, would it be proper for Congress to do what she would not have done? Had the territory in question been located in a free state, and the South had petitioned Congress to admit slaves, or the traffic of slaves in it, contrary to the established usages of the place, would there have been no outcry, no resistance from the North? And would not this very point have been urged, that Congress was transcending its proper limits by doing that which the state having original jurisdiction would never have permitted?

Thirdly. Another circumstance deserving attention is the fact, that probably a majority of the people in the district would at present vote against the interference of Congress on this point: although, while there is so much excitement in the country, no attempt will probably be made to obtain an expression of public sentiment.

Fourthly. I would suggest an opinion, that this district should be held as common ground, on which all the inhabitants of the country may meet on terms of amity. Unhappily, the usages of the various sections of our country are different; on this very account, the central point at which they legislate should be a place where each may find its sectional usages respected. Great forbearance should be exercised, that the people of no section should come here with the feeling, that their rights were infringed or their privileges curtailed. If the sight of a slave is offensive or painful to an abolitionist, he must not only keep away from slavery, but should alter the laws of the United States, which, as a citizen, he is bound to respect; for these recognize the right of carrying slaves all over the country.

Congress has always manifested a very liberal disposition towards this district. It is a beautiful section of hill and dale, well adapted from its locality to be the seat of federal government; and its inhabitants have great reason to be thankful for the liberality and favour of Congress. It has extended a generous hand to aid public improvements, wherever there was a probability of their being useful. It has done much to embellish Washington in its public buildings; and if private enterprise keeps pace with the public munificence, the city cannot fail to be a capital worthy of the Union.

CHAPTER II.

APPEAL TO SLAVEHOLDERS.

I. Design of the writer. Slaveholders and abolitionists ignorant of each other.
II. Character of abolitionists misunderstood — enthusiasts—increased by opposition—many of them well-meaning men.
III. Slavery, general view—negroes human beings, capable of improvement.
IV. Power of the master — slaveholders interrogated. Fearful responsibility in holding human beings as slaves.
V. The Bible on that responsibility.
VI. Brief survey of practical slavery—moral aspect—ignorance—dishonesty, facts in proof—licentiousness, slaveholders aware of the evil.
VII. Influence of slavery on individuals—character of slaves—their influence on masters—on poor white men.
VIII. Influence of slavery on national prosperity—monopoly of cotton—southern system not favourable to improvement—comparison with imperial Rome—with Peru and Mexico.
IX. A better system recommended to the South. Question of moral right will be agitated among slaveholders.
X. Slaveholders plead that a manufacturing country makes actual slaves—some weight in the plea—radical difference. Southern states should depend on agriculture. " Plan " of independence considered.
XI. Views of the North on slavery—tendency of abolition—ridiculous action among some northern manufacturers.
XII. Dissolution of Union threatened—its preservation urged upon the South. North not inimical to the South.
XIII. The probable result of the controversy. Influence of British emancipation. Modern slavery compared with Roman and Grecian. Conclusion.

Slavery—that consuming canker of great states.
SISMONDI.

I. In a former chapter I have given you my views of the measures and movements of abolitionists; permit me now, as a suitable introduction to this, to tell you something of the abolitionists themselves. If the description should differ from the picture in your mind's eye, be assured there is no intentional deception or false colouring; and that it is drawn from actual observation. The writer did not enter upon this undertaking to build up or pull down, to favour or traduce, any party or man, and never entered into any calculation respecting the degree of approbation or censure which might accompany his labours. A good cause never suffered by investigation; a bad one was never permanently benefited by falsehood or intrigue. It is less the design of the writer to give his own opinions, than to state facts, and leave the reader to form his own conclusions.

With these views, it is to be regretted that so much asperity of feeling should exist between the great parties of this controversy—the abolitionists and those slaveholders which have taken a conspicuous part in opposing them—with so little knowledge of each others characters and motives. On each side judgment has been made up from exparte statements, and a verdict rendered against the whole body, from the inflammatory language and excited action of a few. This is not only unhappy, but it might have been prevented by more deliberation and forbearance. It must be most evident that neither party is deserving the unqualified abuse which has been cast upon it by the other.

II. The writer has been personally acquainted with several abolitionists, some of whom have held a prominent place before the public, since the first agitation of the subject; and he is ready to bear witness that they are not the cutthroats and monsters which slaveholders are led to believe. Worse men than they, misguided or unprincipled demagogues, having private interests to subserve or hideous passions to gratify, have raised the hue and cry against them—have set on the mob to break up their meetings, destroy their property, and put their lives in peril—to load them with infamy, and quiet the South. No other result could reasonably be expected, than that which followed. Instead of a handful of quiet, unoffending men, who met to pass resolutions on the subject of slavery, to relieve their minds of a burden, they have grown up, in spite of themselves, into a numerous body; and now occupy a large space in the public mind, both north and south. Sober, reflecting men, who witnessed the treatment they suffered for no illegal act or offence against the laws, necessarily came to the conclusion, that if such violence was to be the penalty of believing and acting as every individual has a right to do, then no man or society would be safe from the exactions and injuries of a lawless infuriated rabble; and they befriended or took sides with the abolitionists, not so much from a belief of their sentiments, as to sustain the peace and order of society.

The men who inflamed the mob and set them

to their task are utterly devoid of principle; and having only selfish purposes to gratify, would as soon set fire to the south as the north, if they could thereby accomplish their interested designs. The miserable beings who generally act as efficient agents in such scenes—men in the likeness but without the attributes of humanity—who have sunk the rational intelligence into brutal vice, and who have brought hopeless poverty and oppression upon themselves in all ages, are probably destined in this, as in every other country, to be controlled, when in masses, like beasts of prey, only by powder and ball. That this class were the *workmen* in these, as in all mobs, there is no doubt; and yet it cannot be denied, that in almost all the tumults growing out of abolition at the North, there have been large numbers of orderly persons, and many respectable citizens, looking on with approbation. If these latter supposed they were aiding in pulling down abolition, by their passive assent in countenancing the mob in pulling down houses, they egregiously erred, as experience has abundantly proved.

True, the abolitionists are enthusiasts—they are absorbed in the contemplation of this, as the great sin of the nation; and believe they are called upon by every principle of Christianity, and by the love of man, to raise their voice against it; and to use every reasonable exertion for its extinction. If they use *unreasonable exertions*, the fault should be attributed in some measure to the headlong precipitancy of the times; and something should charitably be allowed for the infirmities of human nature, under the circumstance in which they have been placed; as all history, civil and ecclesiastical, proves that the proper aliment on which enthusiasm thrives and prospers is *opposition*.

But apart from their exclusiveness on this point, the abolitionists, those of whom the writer can speak from personal experience, are unassuming, peaceable men, having at least as much claim to the character of Christian as their opponents. They would not designedly hurt the hair of the head of a single slaveholder. They have not enlisted in this cause from motives of self-interest, popular favour, or ambition. Were you to sit down with them to discuss the subject of slavery, however the argument might turn, I would guarantee the abolitionist not to be the first to lose temper. Of course, I except certain hotheaded ones, which in this, as in every other cause, are always loaded and primed ready to go off. That many of them are philanthropists, in the highest sense of the term; not giving to those who can repay them, but devoting themselves to seeking out, relieving, and instructing the miserable and wretched, is susceptible of proof. They are actively engaged in some northern cities, in drawing those idle and vagabond children for whom "no man cares" from the streets or their miserable abodes, and collecting and teaching them in Sabbath-schools. For these labours of unrequited philanthropy, of pure, disinterested patriotism, and true charity, I will honour them, and praise them,

—notwithstanding the frowns and scorn of popular obloquy—believing, that in the day which shall "try every man's work, of what sort it is," these labours will stand every test and be approved; whatever may be the fate of their abolition measures.

III. The subject of American slavery is one of such vast magnitude, involving so many interests, and presenting such a variety of aspects, that to trace even an outline of the whole field would require time and research, which the writer is wholly unable to command. He wishes, nevertheless, in the brief space allotted to this chapter, to call your attention to some points of great interest, and deserving your deliberate and profound consideration.

And first, with respect to the main question,— *slavery itself.* It is not necessary to repeat or add to what has been stated in another place. I have there briefly but frankly avowed my own sentiments on the subject. In presenting this appeal to you, I wish as frankly to address you first as accountable beings, and in view of a tribunal hereafter, where the judgments of men will be reviewed and reversed, and where every man will be judged *according to his works.*

I take the ground that the negro is a human being, although now sunk in ignorance, and degraded by slavery—a being, having capacities for improvement and enjoyment above his present lot—a being, accountable to God, and destined to future retribution—and a being who has claims upon the philanthropy of the age, which cannot much longer be slighted or overlooked.

All of you will agree to some of these propositions; some of you will agree to them all. But no efforts for reformation will avail, unless founded upon principles of Christian benevolence. Nothing but the spirit of the gospel can essentially ameliorate the condition, humanize and christianize the negro. All other principles of reformation will degenerate into mercenary and selfish practices. Human nature is essentially the same, in all ages and countries; its great deity is self—its highest attainment self-idolatry.

IV. You hold, by legal possession, by long unquestioned right, the person of the slave. He and his posterity are yours to employ, and to dispose of, according to your own pleasure. His time and abilities are yours—his task has no limit but your will. Of freedom or property he has none. He can make no alliances, no contracts—his wife and children are not his own, but yours. His ignorance and knowledge, his virtue and vice, are governed by the circumstances of his situation. The employment of the faculties which God has given him, and which are indestructible, is influenced by your control; yea, the manner in which he exercises them as an accountable moral being, is shaped by your example and authority.

Now, without entering into any question of right or responsibility, permit me to ask you, on what conditions would you agree to have the order of society reversed, and yourselves and posterity destined to the same state and situation in which you now hold the negro? I do not say, *to* the negro, but in the most favourable circumstances, in which the cases should be parallel; so you would be controlled absolutely by a master, and held " as goods and chattels." Are you indignant at the question? Then there are still stronger reasons for the propriety of asking it. It may not be in accordance with the established rules of fashionable courtesy to propose such a question, as the foundation of an argument or discussion; but in view of the great interests of humanity—of that moral accountability of which we all are partakers—the artificial rules of society will never be permitted to suppress a query, prompted by rectitude of motive, and having for its object an investigation of the utility and propriety of customs and usages practised by a great community.

Perhaps, if you deign an answer, you will summarily decide, that such a reversal is not within the limits of possibility. Were the present state of existence the end of man, this answer might be conclusive, for there is scarcely a possibility that the weak could overcome the strong—that barbarism and ignorance could triumph over civilization and the arts. But this is not the view of the subject we are contemplating. In view of the control you exercise over the slave, do you not sustain the greatest weight of responsibility of which man is susceptible ?—a responsibility greatly increased by being exercised under the light of Christianity. Unless you deny his relation to the human family, you cannot forget that the negro is equally with yourself the creature of the same infinite Creator, —that common Father of all—who is no respecter of persons; and before whom, in all essential attributes, human beings of our race are equal. In the closing hours of life, when the honours, and riches, and colour, which now give you an enviable superiority in the eyes of the world, shall be reduced to their just estimate, this equality will appear with a distinctness which you never imagined. Even, if you are satisfied, beyond the reach of doubt, that slavery in your case is morally right, have you no reason to fear, in view of the frailty and selfishness of our nature, that in the possession of such powers your self-interest or passion will obtain the mastery over reason and conscience— over the perception of right and wrong; and that you will exceed the measure of a rightful and just authority. The rule of that measure is, what you would have exercised over you were you the slave. In view of the moral responsibility attending the condition of master and slave, it appears to me that a man having any adequate perception of that responsibility, and of his own fallibility, would not hesitate, were he destined to choose between them, to *accept the latter*.

I have before stated my belief that slavery to a good master might, by checking the propensities of a debased and groveling human being, prove a blessing. On this point I have adverted to Scripture in proof. Probably every reader of this can immediately refer his thoughts to persons within his knowledge, who would be better off physically, and as far as he can judge morally, in a state of absolute servitude ; such persons, as are now sunk to the lowest point of self-degradation. But would the responsibility of the master cease in such a case ? Certainly not. It must be a law of morals, on which I fear the slaveholder seldom reflects, that the master who consigns a fellow-being to bondage necessarily assumes his responsibilities, so far as he controls him. And if this responsibility is great in respect of the person who has already degraded himself below a consciousness of moral perception; who would willingly incur it in the case of one, possessed of all his faculties, in their full (though untaught) vigour, and who, in favourable circumstances, would assert the dignity and independence of an intelligent free agent.

Slavery must necessarily forbid the development of the mental faculties—the chain which surrounds the body must be drawn so tight as to close every anenue to the mind, or the master would not be secure. If we say the slave has not capacity for greater development or greater enjoyment than he obtains in slavery, we say it in the face of inspiration, which declares that every man shall render an account of the talents committed to his charge. If we bury a single talent belonging to another, which but for our restraint and control would have been improved by the possessor, of us will he demand, to render his account in the day of reckoning.

V. If the Bible teaches us that God permits slavery, it also teaches us the accountability of the master. Nowhere have we more striking proof of the beneficent regard of the Creator for his erring creatures, nor of his endeavors (if the expression be allowable), for the preservation of their liberty and happiness, than in the Mosaic history. Notwithstanding the immediate and frequent revelations which the Almighty gave to the Israelites—the signal interposition of his providence in their deliverance from difficulty—and the impressive obligations resting upon them to deal justly and love mercy—he, their great legislator and guide, who knew the character of man, in his positive institutions for their government, made a provision for their welfare wholly unknown among human legislators, and having a direct bearing upon their social happiness and equal rights. This was the institution of the Jubilee, at which period lands were to revert to their former owners, and slaves to be emancipated. The design of this institution is thus stated, by a learned commentator, forcibly showing the benevolence of the Creator, in providing checks to the natural propensities of men to become tyrants or brutes.

"The reason and design of the Jubilee was partly political and partly typical. It was *political* to prevent too great oppression of the poor, as well as their liability to perpetual slavery. By this means the rich were prevented from accumulating lands upon lands, and a kind of equality was preserved through all the families of Israel. Never was there any people so effectually secure of their liberty and property as the Israelites were, God not only engaging so to protect those invaluable blessings by his Providence, that they should not be taken away from them by others, but providing in a particular manner by this law, that they should not be thrown away through their own folly, since the property which every man or family had in their dividend of the land of Canaan could not be sold or any way alienated, for above half a century."*

Every reader of the books of Moses must be struck with the following reflections:—

First. That God intended the Israelites to be equal in rights and privileges. All had an equal interest in the division of the land of Canaan, according to their families and numbers. No king was appointed over them. Moses was merely a deputy lawgiver under the Almighty, and the heads

* Horne's Introduction, Art. Jubilee.

of tribes were honored as counsellors, without any superior share in the inheritance. It was a pure republic, with provisions for its welfare and permanence such as infinite wisdom only could make.

Second. Slavery (from among the heathen) was tolerated, but under positive restrictions of not more than fifty years' continuance; at which period also, lands sold were to revert to the original proprietors.

Third. The melancholy proof of the depravity and impiety of human nature,—in so soon forgetting the awful manifestations of Deity, by which the giving of these laws was solemnized—in neglecting that reverence and love of God, which a sense of his goodness and protection should have kept burning in their hearts—and, finally, in violating his positive commands, and utterly disregarding the penalty annexed, thus daring the execution of that penalty, which they have suffered to the uttermost, and under the doom of which they remain to this day.

In connection with this it may be observed, that the most fearful judgments, perhaps, in the whole Bible, are denounced against oppressors; those who grind the face of the poor, and withhold from the hireling his due. The most grievous calamities, and especially the scattering of the Jews among all nations, (Jer. xxxiv.) are particularly threatened for their oppression, in not giving the freedom promised and ordained in the law of Moses. How far these threatenings are applicable to modern slavery, is a question which fallible men should be cautious in determining.

VI. I purpose now to take a brief survey of slavery, with regard to its moral and political aspect; for this is the only sure test of utility in every human institution. I will not designedly overcolour the picture, nor give it a single hue which reality will not sanction. Every man, however humble, exerts an influence on society for good or evil; and every writer probably adds something to the aggregate of human happiness or misery. In this belief, I would write nothing without a deep-felt consciousness, that the eye of Omniscience is upon me, and that for my words and sentiments, and their influence upon the world, an account must be rendered.

And first, the moral aspect of slavery as it is developed in our own country. On this subject I have no wish to go into detail. I will state some of those prominent facts, which are known and read of all men in a slave country—submitting to those interested to judge the fairness of the statements, and leaving the reader to draw his own conclusions. The first question touching the morals of a community, is in respect to its religion. And the slaves as a body must be without intelligent piety, for they are without any learning. The laws generally—and I know not but in all the states—interdict their being taught to read; and even when it may perhaps be left to the discretion of the master, the result is essentially the same.

Ignorance is always an attendant upon slavery. Yet, while every advocate or apologist of slavery must admit the necessity of this, enlightened piety must deplore the consequences, in regarding them as accountable beings. Reading is emphatically the key of knowledge, and how ministers and Christians can reconcile with the precepts of the Bible, their taking away this key from one-half the community of human beings, is beyond my comprehension. A land of Bibles, and one-half the immortal souls not permitted to read it! We deplore the biblical ignorance of the people in popish countries—ought we not to lament the moral darkness of our own? Surely Christian slavery gives the strongest evidence of man's corruption and depravity, for it virtually declares these to be more influential in governing men than the Bible.

Hence the slave, whose only knowledge of religion is derived from example and oral instruction, forms his estimate of its value from its practical influence upon those around him. I fear this reflected light from example would be so feeble, even from the most pious community in the Union, as to be but a very uncertain guide to the ignorant. There are many persons in the south, who take an active interest in the subject, and devote much time to the oral instruction of the negro; and no doubt the ministers of the gospel generally encourage and assist in the work: but whether they discharge all their duty to the slave, must be left to Omniscience to decide. Very many of the slaves in the large towns are regular attendants upon worship, and communicants in the church; and most of the masters in the country encourage their slaves to attend: and although the number of attendants in the country, so far as the writer's observation extended, is small, he has been informed that this is by no means generally the case. Some masters practically encourage the desecration of the Sabbath, by requiring six days' labour of the slaves; thus leaving them only the seventh for the cultivation of their own garden, and the performance of other necessary duties; but by far the greater number give them a portion of time expressly for their own services and duties, and most of these also discountenance their labouring on the Sabbath.

Another feature characteristic of southern slavery is dishonesty—perhaps I should say pilfering—and its sure concomitant, lying. Two facts which are peculiar to the south will prove this statement.

First, almost every house is guarded by one or more dogs—generally a pack—a great nuisance to the traveller who is unaccustomed to such society—extremely savage, and especially taught to seize the negro in his night maraudings.

Secondly, every mistress or housekeeper in town and country keeps her rooms locked, forbidding entrance without permission. This practice appears to be reduced to a system, and vigilantly attended to; thus giving evidence that the danger is not from without, as in cities, but from within. It seems to be a household maxim, that servants are not to be trusted. Having no liberty, no property of his own, is it surprising that the slave should cove, and in his moral and mental ignorance appropriate to his own use, something of the abundance which surrounds him, or whatever accident throws in his way, that may minister to his gratification? Naturally of a social disposition, but denied by his situation from enjoying his propensity during the day, his nights are frequently given to visiting, frolicking, rambling, plundering.

But the darkest moral feature in the South is licentiousness. It walks like the pestilence at noonday—lurks in every corner and by-way at night—and nothing is free from its contamination. I am satisfied but few slaveholders themselves know the amount of this vice carried on among them. Sensuality is a strong propensity in the negro, and in his state of degradation, and in the absence of mental pleasures, it is not wonderful that sensual indulgence should have a strong dominion over him. Besides, it cannot be questioned, that this vice is often practically encouraged by his white superiors; and where every tie of family kindred is liable to be broken at the will of the master—where the slave is permitted to have no individual will, but is personally and mentally subjected—where passive acquiescence to the demands or wishes of a superior may prove a source of mitigation of evils—where all these are combined with the natural inclination of the negro, what can prevent a flood of pollution from pouring over the land. Nothing can prevent it, but a strong sense of moral principle; and whether a state of domestic slavery is more or less favourable to the formation and exertion of such a principle, is submitted to the consideration of slaveholders. From impressions on the mind of the writer, he is confident that a little observation and inquiry will give such a view of the subject, as to make a moral man ashamed that he belongs to the species. Pen should not write, a virtuous mind should not for a moment retain expressions of deeds, of which men, called respectable, openly boast.

And a southern slaveholder never ought to utter a word of reproach, or speak of amalgamation, in connection with the free states. Were every black there to be married to a white, the result would not exhibit such a motley complexion, as the South now presents, in open defiance of every moral and religious precept. The one might offend the established rules of society; the other outrages every sentiment of decency. You may very frequently at the South see a black woman with two or three children, each of a different coloured hue—such things pass without observation as a matter of course. And I have sometimes while traveling, asked the question respecting a fellow-being before me, "is that man black or white?" The answer was generally, "he is a slave." And I need not allude to the endless variety of shades which meet the eye, in observing the coloured population, in all the cities of the south. Leaving out of view entirely, the idea of moral responsibility, what are the prospects of such a state of society? Who can be secure, when the very atmosphere is loaded with pestilence? Who can be surrounded with fire, and not be scorched? What an introduction to manhood, have the youth of such a society!

I know that many persons at the south, many slaveholders, view this picture of society with dismay, and are anxiously looking for some ray of light to break in upon the surrounding darkness. They know that it is poisoning the fountains of morals, and undermining the very foundations of society. They know also that slavery is the procuring cause of the evil, by placing the cup within the reach of every individual, and that public opinion silently acquiesces in the practice. In the frontier states, these men have hope of removing the evil by destroying the cause; but in the far south, where self-interest, worldly prosperity, the climate and habits of society, combine to perpetuate slavery, some of these men do not hesitate to express a belief, that slavery is destined to take a terrible revenge—not by insurrection, but by amalgamation—the black swallowing up the white.

VII. Secondly.—The influence of slavery, with respect to individual and national prosperity, were there no other objection to slavery, I would urge emancipation upon the master from motives of *political economy* alone. No country or state ever was or can be permanently prosperous, where the mass of the population are slaves. That slavery is contrary to the original designs of the Creator, and the established laws which govern the world of mind, is sufficiently proved from its unprofitableness. We need not appeal to history or human science for the proof of these propositions. That slave-labour is necessarily unproductive, must be evident to the most common reflection. As a general principle, with rare exceptions, no man will exert himself to do any thing without an object in prospect, and every man's exertion and perseverance will be in proportion to the value he places upon that object. Now, on this common sense principle, what motive has the slave to labour? He is a mere passive instrument in the hands of another: he has no voice in the direction, no profit in the result of his labour: he will have his food and clothing, although the cattle destroy the corn; he will have no more, although it yields an hundred fold.*

He has no attachment to the soil except from

---

* Upon reading this chapter to a slaveholder from an agricultural district, he objected to the above, stating, that in his neighbourhood, there was a very manifest rivalry among the slaves of different plantations, to make the best crop of cotton, and a feeling of pride among those that succeeded. I very cheerfully give his statement a place, and should be happy to learn that the same was true of the slave states extensively.

habit; and the force of his application is a compact between his sluggish indifference and the value he sets upon the ill or good will of his master. He has no motive to be saving or economical; for every thing around him belongs to another. He is a machine impelled by extraneous force—just like a watch, which will *go* as long as it is wound up; and, like a watch, the slave must be wound up every day; he must have his orders daily, and must have a command repeated every time a certain service is required, although it may be only " to water the horse," or " shut the gate." His want of care, his negligence and forgetfulness, are complete—established traits of character. Of consequence, a great deal of his labour, inefficient as it is, is unproductive, or rendered of no avail.

It is a common remark of those persons acquainted with slave-labour, and northern free-labour, that their proportion is as one to two. This is not too great an estimate in favour of the free labourer; and the circumstances of their situation produce a still greater disparity. The absence of motive, and the consequent want of mental energy to give vigor to the arm of the slave, is the source of another great drawback upon the usefulness of his labour. His implements or tools are at least one-third (in some instances more than twofold) heavier and stronger than the northern man's, to counteract his want of skill and interest in his work. A negro hoe or scythe would be a curiosity to a New England farmer. Of course the extra exertion required in the use of these tools, is a deduction from the profit of his labour. All his manufacturing and repairing, except regular tradesmen, of which there are some respectable workmen at the South, are of the rudest kind ; and a northern man, seeing his heavy cart attached to a mule, with the relics of a harness, kept together by cords and straps, is at once led to reflect upon the probable advancement the American negro has made in mechanical ingenuity over his brethren on the banks of the Goliba.

There is another view of this subject to be taken also, in the light of political economy; and that is the influence of slavery upon the white population. Some writer has said " every man is as lazy as he can be ;" but the remark should be taken with the same limitation as that, in which the inspired Psalmist called " all men liars ;" he said it " in his haste." Notwithstanding, there is one denunciation in the Bible, which mankind, in all ages and countries, have regarded with peculiar dislike, and used all their efforts to shun. There is indeed, comparatively, a few who have looked upon this denunciation as a blessing in disguise, and have therefore cheerfully acquiesced in it ; but their number has always been so small, and they themselves adjudged by the world to be a class of old-fashioned, mean-spirited beings, that they have made very few converts to their faith or practice. The passage alluded to may be found in one of the first chapters of Genesis, and reads thus—" in the sweat of thy face shalt thou eat bread," which in modern paraphrase is generally understood to mean, "thou shalt work for a living." Of all the punishments inflicted or threatened upon man by his Creator, this appears to be regarded as the greatest, and men have exercised every ingenuity to escape it.

But there is no reason to believe that southern men or slaveholders are sinners above all others in this respect; for the New Englander has at heart as great a horror of the spade and hoe: but the former has a great advantage over the latter in situation, being supplied with a plenty of other hands, in the sweat of whose faces, instead of his own, he eats bread. The wealthy planter need not work, and does not, neither does the wealthy northern farmer. On lands fertile in soil, and large in extent, he can bid defiance to Franklin's maxim,—

"Whoever by the plough would thrive,
Himself must either hold or drive"—

as he has one or two grades of officers between himself and the labourer; and therefore takes but little interest in the detail of his great estate. Between these proprietors of the first class, and those whites who are absolutely poor, there are a number of grades which, in proportion to the quality of their lands and the number of their slaves, are enabled to live more or less at their ease, in respect to worldly competence. But most of these take some direct and daily interest in the management of their estates.

A class of these, in moderate rather than affluent circumstances, probably enjoy life with more real satisfaction, than any other. With a few negroes, not more than they can personally superintend, and not enough to preclude the necessity of their constant supervision, and assistance in labour—they work almost as regular and perseveringly as the New England farmer. Many of this class are also wise enough to bring their sons up to labour—take them into the field, and put them side by side with the slave. This is the most virtuous and truly independent class of southern men, the true lords of the soil—the strong framework of society. In all these classes, except perhaps the highest, the negligence and carelessness of the negro requires a degree of vigilance, and causes an amount of anxiety, which makes a large deduction from the ease of the master.

And besides, the fixed habits of the negro have exerted a powerful influence to the master's injury. The latter seems from a kind of necessity to have accommodated himself to the slovenly course of the slave. There appears to be a great want of method, and destitution of energy in almost every thing about him. His inclosed fields are too large for profitable culture; his pastures generally open in commons; his fences rude and out of repair; and his buildings and tools, and vehicles, not of the best construction for available profit. There is an appearance of want of thrift generally, which strikes an observer from the old states of the north, as evidence that there is *some cause operating extensively against the inhabitants, preventing them from reaping the natural benefits of their situation, with respect to climate, soil, and local advantages.*

But there is another class of whites, equal perhaps to all the others in number, upon which slavery has had an indirect but decided influence. In a country where slaves perform all or nearly all the work, it cannot be expected that labour will be considered respectable; and this public sentiment of the rich operates with fatal influence upon the energy of the poor man. By a poor man is meant one too indigent to own slaves. As a general fact, they are unwilling to be hired, to go into the field with the slave. Some of them are overseers or managers for the planters, a situation I believe in which few accumulate property. Many of them possess considerable tracts of land (which is very cheap) from which, in the vicinity of navigable waters, they carry considerable quantities of wood to market. Many of them near the large towns are small gardeners, others are sailors, boatmen, fishermen,—while great numbers probably depend more on their dogs and guns, and female industry, for support, than any regular business. As a body, so far as the writer can judge, the class of poor whites are ignorant. Great numbers even in the Old Dominion can neither read nor write. In this respect, however, there is a better prospect for the children. And I need not prove, that as a body, the poor class of whites in the slave states are vicious, if rum drinking, profanity, and laziness entitle men to that appellation. To what extent the effects here spoken of are to be attributed to slavery, must be left for others to decide.

VIII. I shall probably be met here with the assertion, that the South, even with its slave labour, produces three fourths of all the exports of the country; and shall be asked how this fact is reconcilable with the wastefulness of that labour, and the poverty it tends to produce.

This will bring us to a consideration of the influence of slavery, in respect to political economy. The fact is conceded, that the states of the South produce most of the exports of the nation in numerical amount; but it does not thence follow, that these states are adding to individual and national prosperity in the same proportion. Slavery and slave labour are inherently the same in all parts of the world, but various circumstances modify their influence in different states and countries. In Alabama and Louisiana slave labour is more valuable than in Virginia—not because the slave is more industrious or less wasteful—but because the articles he produces are more profitable. In many parts of Virginia, a slave in cultivating corn will hardly produce his own support; take the same slave to Mississippi, and with the same time and exertion of labour in producing cotton, he would be worth annually several hundred dollars clear profit. Evidently then, the advantage is not in the slave, but in his situation.

The South, from its local position, possesses a monopoly of one of the greatest staples of traffic in the commercial world. Its virgin soil produces cotton in abundance, and the demand for the article in all the manufacturing districts of Europe and America, in this age of universal peace, and improvements in the arts, sustains a price which affords an enormous profit. It has been stated that the labour of a slave in producing cotton or sugar, would in two or three years amount to his value, 1000 or 1500 dollars.

Much is said at this day about national prosperity, but without definition, it is a mere abstract term, and has no political meaning. If by national prosperity is meant, the useful and profitable employment of all the individuals of a nation; and at the same time suitable provision for increase of population, then the expression has a very significant meaning. If the individuals of a nation are prosperous, it will be a prosperous nation of course. That the cotton states produce national prosperity in this sense, by adding to the profitable employment of individuals, is very true; but the least part of this prosperity is realized at the south. Let us enter into an examination of this statement. In conformity with southern usage, we shall consider the whites alone as population or individuals, leaving the slaves entirely out of view, as passive agents, or mere cattle. Now, how the planter can be said to be usefully or profitably employed—in cultivating a square mile of cotton with 200 labourers,—thus absorbing the means of sustaining 100 individuals, I do not see. With all this estate he can live in but one house, eat and drink, and sleep for one, and enjoy life only as an individual. True, he may travel, possess fine equipages, be clothed like a prince, and spend money like a prodigal—but this does not improve his land, add to his resources, nor make room for an increase of population.

Again, the cotton which *he* produces (without other human agents) is carried to New or Old England, and in the process of manufacture employs 100 persons, or 20 families; each of which must have a house to live in; and must have food and clothing, giving useful employment to many others. Now which possesses the greatest resources of prosperity, the plantation of the cotton cultivator, or the place (suppose the same extent of territory) where the cotton is manufactured? The former contains a population of one or two families, and one or two houses; the latter contains a population of twenty families, in twenty houses, with plenty of vacant room for more, the price of which is continually advancing, as new houses are called for: as the number of manufacturing operatives is increased, the demand for other mechanics is extended, and the increased consumption of agricultural products greatly enhances the value and price of land.

Now let us enlarge the scale, without changing the principle. On ten thousand square miles of territory are five thousand cotton planters—assuming that the cotton land of each is one half of his estate or plantation—having splendid houses to live in—immensely rich—and with every luxury at command which money will purchase, or man has a capacity to enjoy. On the other hand, on ten thousand square miles are forty thousand families, and although not living in the same splendour—usefully and profitably employed. In the latter case, the activity of the people, and the increase and facilities of business invite population; the very circumstances of the former repel it. Now which of these communities adds most to the wealth and strength of a nation? In case of war, which would most likely be attacked? That where wealth was concentrated in a few hands, or that where conquest would afford the least plunder in proportion to the inhabitants, and where an attack would be opposed by a greater force? In which of these communities will there probably be the greatest improvement and skill in the useful arts: the most activity, industry, and physical and mental energy? Which of them will most probably establish and sustain schools, and become an intelligent community?

If the foregoing contrast is founded on facts and reason, the southern planter may see the direct tendency and result of the system on which he acts. His productions are a source of great national prosperity (in a nation so extensive and various as ours), but unfortunately they benefit himself and his part of the nation the least.* The cotton states *add immensely more to the wealth, resources, and strength of England, than they do to themselves*—but this is no fault of the former, rather their own. She is pursuing a course which invites an increase of active population; and which gives momentum and energy to every branch of industry—every department of science; *they repel such population.* Hence they pay an exorbitant tax for the services of transient mechanics and merchants, who retire to spend their profits elsewhere. The grand secret is the difference in their

---

* The aggregate of southern exports is immense in annual amount—so many millions for cotton—so many for rice, sugar, and tobacco. But it is easily demonstrable that the amount of northern *agricultural production*, independent of her commerce and manufactures, exceeds that of the South, even in proportion to her population. This is true of the two sections taken as a whole, or of any particular portions compared together. For instance, the annual amount of production of western New-York or Ohio, from the forest, the grass and grain fields, the pastures and gardens, will exceed the amount from an equal territory, selected from any portion of the South. The great difference is, the productions of the latter are sent abroad, while those of the latter are consumed at home; and, therefore, not so tangible or visible, except in the progressive improvement, and rise and accumulation of property in the immediate section itself.

systems. The manufacturing country (if free) must *necessarily* expand itself. The system of the South will *not bear* expansion.

And this system is alike unfavourable to the development of internal resources, of physical and moral power. With their monopoly of products, and fertility of soil, the states of the South ought to be the richest in the world. Those on the Gulf of Mexico possess a mine in these respects, which might produce wealth enough to plate their surface with silver. But the blessings of Providence are poured into their lap in such profusion, that frail human nature is incapable of making the best use of them. They spend their immense incomes in personal accomplishments, in personal enjoyments, in lordly munifience. Each man is for himself, living and enjoying in his isolated grandeur; never dreaming that there is any bottom to the fertility of his soil, or limit to his pleasures. His individual (personal) prosperity is apparently unbounded and enviable. But it is delusive. He is, politically, like a man in a balloon, sailing at an amazing elevation above the rest of the world, but liable every moment to be dashed down to earth. His children are not so likely to be taught the value of time, of money, of character, of morals, of physical energy. One certain result of that indolence and luxurious mode of living, consequent upon the sudden influx and increase of wealth in a family or state, is to effeminate the physical powers, deteriorating man more and more in every successive generation.

Rome in her richest days was in similar circumstances to the states enjoying this monopoly, and she sunk under the burden. Central Italy was too much occupied in war, and her freemen were too proud to labour, while the necessaries and luxuries of life were profusely supplied by the distant provinces. These, although possessed by the wealthy patricians of Rome, were cultivated by slaves so degraded and brutalized, as to offer no resistance even to barbarian invaders. Hence, between the luxurious effeminacy of the masters, and the despicable condition of the labourers, the empire became an easy and an inviting prey.

But a more exact parallel may be drawn between these states and the mining countries of Mexico and South America. So utterly subversive of all moral principle, and all physical energy, is the acquisition of great wealth without personal effort, that these countries, although possessing the very fountains of *money*—whence the streams flow all over the world—are among the weakest in power, and the most abandoned in morals: while the passion for gold, absorbing all other passions and interests, has entirely paralysed the energies of the mother country, and in two centuries, almost completely prostrated one of the proudest and most powerful states in Christendom. I do not say the South would ever descend so low in the scale of moral and mental degradation as these states—it is in a great measure free from their ignorance, and from the influence of a corrupt, irresponsible priesthood ; but the tendency of its system—the accumulation of the wealth of the state—and that wealth immense in comparatively a few hands, is precisely the same; and, unless human nature is changed, must lead to the same result.

IX. Now, permit me to ask the southern planter if it would not be better for him, better for his state and section, better for the nation, and better in *every point of view*, to divide his twelve hundred acres, or two square miles of land, into farms of one hundred acres each, and farm it out to twelve men or families. By giving them long leases (on the English system), these tenants would have a direct interest in preserving the fertility of the rich, and replenishing the exhausted soils; and by actual personal inspection of the whole—and that prudent economical management which men generally exercise *in their own concerns*—greatly increase the amount of production. If, by this means, the planter should obtain the same income from his estate that he does at present, and at the same time his estate should support twelve other industrious families, would he not enhance the value of his own property, and add to the resources of his community?

By being relieved of the responsibility and anxiety of watching and directing one or two hundred idle, wasteful, and refractory hands, would he not be happier? As long as he remains isolated in his present situation, he cannot improve his property. He will wear out and exhaust, but will not replenish. He will be behind the age in constructing internal improvements for the public good. Old Virginia will show him by ocular proof the inevitable result of his own system. She practised it on a soil, perhaps somewhat originally inferior to that of Alabama, and a hundred and fifty years has exhausted her entirely. Let him go to the North, and examine the condition of the same extent of land as his own plantation,—see the number of inhabitants on it—the industrious competition continually active—and he may at once see the reason why real estate is continually advancing in all the old free states, and actually declining in the old settled parts of the slave states. He may easily tell the reason why Massachusetts, with its bogs, and rocks, and cold climate, would sell in market for more money than old Virginia, with her double population, her eightfold extent, her navigable waters, and unrivalled situation. Let him compare their systems of operation, and he will see further, that if the population of Massachusetts were placed in Virginia, it would, in a few years, resuscitate the exhaustion of her maritime section, tunnel her mountains to the Ohio, and bring to light the inexhaustible mineral wealth hidden in her interior. He would see, that one-fourth of the population of Virginia, carrying with them the Virginia system, spread all over the former state, would soon perish with famine.

In stating this contrast, I have made but slight reference to the question of *morals*, or of *human rights*. But they must enter deeply into every question affecting the welfare of society. That luxury and pride, idleness and haughty independence, almost certainly follow the acquisition of sudden wealth, requires no proof. Impiety to God, and hard-heartedness to man, follow in the train. That the morals of the South are not too deeply imbued with that spirit of meekness and forbearance which the Bible inculcates, is evident from the number of gentlemanly assassinations in affrays and duels which so frequently occur. With regard to human rights, there are some persons who would be inclined to ask in their simplicity whether it is *right* for one man to make two hundred fellow-beings, (perhaps as honest, as virtuous, as capable of improvement as himself), labour, that he may spend their earnings according to his pleasure. And the time will come when this question will be asked at the South, not in corners and whispers, but openly and loudly, and *all over the South*. And the social agitation which will accompany this inquiry, will give the people new eyes to see things, which, although lying on the very surface of society, unyielding prejudice has hither prevented them from seeing. I invoke the hastening of this period from motives of sincere regard for the best interests and welfare of the South.

X. And here, I am aware the slaveholder may, perhaps, plead the unfairness of this contrast so far as slavery is concerned, and contend that the manufacturing section, when densely populated, will produce a class of labourers, poor, ignorant, and debased—slaves in every thing but the name. Candour must admit that this plea is not without weight. *It has weight.* The tendency of large manufactories is the same as large slave plantations, viz. to absorb the wealth of the state, and place it in a few hands. And whenever the manufacturers should outnumber the agricultural population, the result would be a controlling influence of an irresponsible, wealthy aristocracy. Experience proves that the influence of manufacturing upon labourers is bad; as a class they are exceedingly improvident, and the peculiar circumstances of their situation, fosters ignorance, licentiousness, and intemperance. In view of this, the legislatures of some of the states have enacted laws compelling the education of the children. By banishing ardent spirits, also, the rapid descent of this class to abject poverty and degradation will be arrested. But as soon as the demand for manufacturing labourers shall be exceeded by the supply, competition will reduce the wages to a bare subsistence, and then the employer will control the labourer, almost without responsibility: for what is now common, viz. so great a degree of poverty, as to be unable to remove a family from one factory to another, will then be nearly universal. Nothing but law and public opinion will then interpose in favour of the labourer, and these have always been a very feeble barrier to wealthy aggression. If the remark of an English manufacturer to the writer is to be credited, the females in the English factories are as much in the power of *their masters* as the southern slave, and perhaps as vicious.

And yet at the worst, there is an immeasurable distance between the slave and free labourer. The former is entirely passive, the latter voluntary. No ray of mental light can reach the slave. If he could *see* his chains, he would make an effort to break them. But the freeman has liberty to rise, and may surmount the hardships of his state, and become a prominent man in society. The institutions of the state, and public sentiment, both invite him to educate his children. There is no obligation to hinder him from leaving his employment at any moment, but such as he has imposed upon himself. If he is not a slave to vice, the most grievous of all slavery, there is always hope of his rising in the world. Actual slavery destroys its victim at once, and is no worse in generations—but the descent and degradation of the free labourer is gradual, and is frequently a long period in reaching its ultimate depression. I cannot conceive an obtuseness of intellect so great, as not to perceive a radical difference between the two cases.

But there is no necessity or propriety in drawing a comparison between the slave and the manufacturing labourer. I bespeak no indulgence, and shun no responsibilities, in declaring (from actual knowledge of both) that the lower class of whites at the South are as poor, as ignorant, as vicious, to say the least, as the labouring operatives in the northern manufactories. Taken as an average, as a body, or as individuals, the latter will not suffer in comparison.

In leaving this part of the subject, I wish to make a few observations to prevent misapprehensions respecting what has been stated of the southern system of labour.

Nothing in the foregoing remarks was intended to bear, in the least, against the great business of the South—but against the mode of conducting it. The Almighty Disposer, who allots to men their destiny in this life, has evidently designed these states to be agricultural; and in their fertility, facilities of production, and in a monopoly of cotton, they are indebted to Him for a source of wealth, an amount and aggregate of profit, which no other community ever possessed. They only need to avail themselves of the best plan of operations for applying their resources to this business, to be immensely rich and powerful. The product is immense, and so is the profit: both might be increased. But it would seem they are dissatisfied with their circumstances, and aim at grasping the business of their northern neighbours. Let them be reminded of the fable—" of the dog carrying the meat over the river." If I were an enemy to the South, I would encourage the "*plan*" to render themselves "independent of the North," by exporting their own produce and importing their own goods. That they can buy goods as cheap in England or France, as northern merchants, cannot be doubted; but that they can build ships and carry on commerce, and diffuse foreign merchandize through the interior, as cheap as can be done at the North, is out of the question, unless they can anticipate a period of fifty years; for to this amount of time, the North are ahead of them, *in these respects:* and it is but a poor compliment to themselves, to suppose the North has any design of injuring the South, in her manufactures or commerce. The North was driven to extend her interest in these by the force of circumstances. The poverty of her soil, and the severity of her climate compelled her increasing population to seek other channels of active business; and it was only by perseverance against obstacles, and by a gradual progress, that her commerce and manufactures reached their present elevation. The increase of these, naturally led to the construction of canals and railroads. But none of these great enterprizes can be successfully carried on without a dense population. This is also necessary, in order to develop the internal resources of a state. Has the South so far extended her cultivation, that she can spare labourers to dig the ore and work iron, to build ships, to man them, to manufacture goods, which she now receives from the North? If not, then she will not succeed any better in extending her commerce and manufactures, than would the middle states, in endeavouring to cultivate their own cotton. Each would be out of the sphere in which Providence evidently designed it to act. But perhaps the South *covet the profits* of the North. Let them rather take good care of their own. I am no merchant, but will guaranty that the importers, ship owners, manufacturers, and merchants of New York, will exchange profits on the capital invested in their employments. for the profits on an equal amount invested in cotton cultivation. If the South are fearful of becoming "dependent" let them make the proposition. This "plan" before mentioned seems to be started as an offsett to northern abolition. The scheme is entirely worthy of that which gave it birth: and I cannot but hope and believe, for the best good of the country, and the whole country, that either will be discountenanced and abandoned before it involves its own section of the Union in disaster and distress.

XI. It may not be improper, after giving my views of slavery and slaveholding, to offer the South some information respecting the state of public sentiment at the North. On this point, a right understanding is of immense importance. A spirit of jealousy and suspicion is awakened in each section of the Union, leading to crimination and threatening; and this arises chiefly from ignorance of each other's views and circumstances. It was a principal object of the writer in commencing this appeal, to remove this ignorance, and if possible make the great mass of the people on each side better acquainted with each other. If this is effected, there is hope that the question may be amicably settled. I have often thought it must be difficult for the people of the South to form any correct opinion of northern feeling on this subject, from the various and contradictory statements of the press. One will aver that abolitionits are silenced : another will declare they are increasing. One states that the North is sound on this subject, and the slaveholder has nothing to fear ; another comes out boldly, and connecting the subject of free discussion, declares that the North are all for abolition.

The fact is, the free states, *as a people*, have not yet spoken on this subject. They are a deliberate, thinking community, not easily excited ; and there is no great question of universal and absorbing interest like slavery among them, to draw out public sentiment. I will venture, as an individual, to make two statements, as facts, respecting the people of the free states.

First. They generally, almost universally, hold slavery in abhorrence. This is the settled feeling and conviction of their hearts. They believe it to be cruel wrong to the slave, and as far as they have information, believe it to be deeply injurious to the masters. These are their views respecting slavery in the abstract—slavery everywhere. These are the reasons which influenced them to abolish it among themselves, and which will always determine them to reject it.

Second. I believe there is a firmly settled conviction, that it would be wrong for them to take any steps to *enforce abolition* at the South. In addition to their convictions of a moral nature on this subject, there is a very general belief that in the compact of our government, slavery was fairly though tacitly recognized, and left to the exclusive control and action of the several states respectively. Just in this position they are now inquiring what is their duty with respect to any action on the subject; and even if the South should now dissolve the Union, they would still inquire and deliberate, although that event would probably hasten their decision, and also, probably change its character.

If asked, whether abolition is increasing, I should answer, yes.* The numerous abolition societies,

---

* Since the above was written, circumstances have taken place which require the answer to this question to be somewhat modified. For a year past, the mobbing of abolitionists has been a rare occurrence, and so far as the limited observation of the writer has extended, the consequences have not been favourable to the growth of immediate abolition. The cause of that incitement, which persecution always gives to a feeble party in a free, intelligent community, being thus removed, the abolitionists appear to be falling out among themselves, and earnestly intent upon discovering the true Solomons of the party. It is to be hoped for the honour of our country, and the cause of free discussion, that such disgraceful scenes will no more be enacted. If left to stand or fall on their own merits, the good sense of the people will

and the increase of petitions to Congress, are sufficient evidence of the fact; but there is no proof in this that the North will ever attempt to force abolition. Nor is there any proof within the knowledge of the writer, that any abolitionists have this object in view. As a body they entirely disclaim it. Some of the most elevated men in the free states, elevated as Christians, as statesmen, as philanthropists, men who are favourably known on both sides of the Atlantic, are decided abolitionists in sentiment, and unequivocally disclaim the thought. The abolitionists disclaim the use of any weapons but those of persuasion and moral force. They have adopted the plan of affiliated societies, which is one of the peculiar features of the age, and adopted by all sorts of interests. As a means of spreading their sentiments, and enlightening public opinion, they employ agents to lecture on the subject, and distribute their publications. They take the ground, that every subject among a free people is open to investigation—that it is evidence of a bad cause to shun the light—and that good institutions are never afraid to have the foundation on which they stand thoroughly examined. When questioned respecting their object, they answer that public opinion requires to be enlightened on the subject. When the North is brought to view slavery in its proper light—in other words, as they

pass a verdict upon the measures of the abolitionists, which, whether it be condemnation or approval, will be final; and in that verdict every good citizen will acquiesce.

view it—they expect that its influence will be felt with such weight at the South as to procure voluntary abolition.

In all this, there is nothing illegal, and if left to themselves, public sentiment at the North will pass a righteous verdict upon their designs and measures. But their numbers have been increased, and their influence extended by the short-sighted zeal and the reproaches of their opponents. Persecution has added tenfold to their societies, and has brought the subject home to the reflection of tenfold more who never gave it reflection. It is astonishing that the light of all history should be lost upon the present age. Persecution never failed in a free country to build up a sect or party, which differed from the majority in matters of opinion not amenable to the laws. I should fear the spread of Mohammedanism, in this country, were one of that belief located among us to be ridiculed and persecuted, because he chose to pray in the streets with his face towards Mecca.

Apply these observations to facts respecting abolitionists. Look at New York, Boston, and Utica, where the violence of mobs was put in requisition to break up their meetings. In all these places they have increased tenfold, and can now meet, and say, and do what they please, and publish their proceedings without fear. It is a principle of republicanism, which the North will adhere to, while she is worthy of freedom, that truth and error are to be left to combat each other in open field.

While on this subject, I wish to disabuse the South on one point. The great excitement in the slave states, a few years ago, was followed by meetings in various parts of the North, disclaiming all connection with the abolitionists, and denouncing them as disunionists, disturbers of the peace, &c. This was one of the most ridiculous farces ever enacted in a civilized community. The ostensible object was to convince the South that the North was not hostile to slavery; the real design was to save the southern market, for the sale of patent yankee notions. The writer is acquainted in some of the places where these patriotic meetings were held, and he doubts not if the views of the persons assembled had been honestly expressed, the preambles to their resolutions would have commenced with the speech of the silversmith of Ephesus, (Acts xxv. 19)—whereas, " sirs, ye know that, by this craft, we have our wealth." Every high-minded man will respect those manufacturers more (and such there are), who are open, avowed abolitionists.

XII. Much has been said and written between the North and South, since this controversy began, respecting its ultimate tendency; and the separation of the Union has been repeatedly and loudly threatened. This subject will be noticed in a future page; but I beg the privilege of offering a few suggestions on this head for the reflection of southern men—leaving to their judgment, both the wisdom of the suggestions and the motives which prompted them.

The threatenings alluded to have generally come from the South, and some persons have been led to fear that the country was rapidly verging to such a catastrophe. But recent observation has convinced me that many northern men are making up their minds to this event, and that the North will accept the dissolution, *if it must come*, without reluctance. From such a period to our national union, may Heaven preserve us.

But the most important suggestion I have to offer the South, is—*preserve the Union*, preserve it at any sacrifice. I do not hesitate to say, preserve it at the expense of slavery. It will be the less of two evils. It is for your interest, at least as much as for the North, to preserve it. Both sections might undoubtedly exist as independent nations, but they could not long exist in peace. Neither individuals nor communities can be aware of the ultimate consequences of measures adopted in times of great excitement. Suffer no sudden ebullition of feeling to commit acts which cannot be rescinded, or to take steps which cannot be retraced. A subject of greater importance, more deeply, perhaps vitally, affecting the best interests of man, probably never agitated the world. Before deciding upon declaring or even accepting a separation of the Union, look into futurity, and ponder the result. *Be sure that the great objects, for which you would barter the Union, would be attained.* The South cannot avoid an investigation of the merits of slavery. Whether welcome or not, she must grapple the public opinion of the age on this question. Can she go through this struggle *alone*, better than as a co-equal branch of the Union? Again, will disunion give security to the possession of her slaves in peace? These are points which should be deeply and thoroughly weighed.

A breach like this, once effected, can never be healed. As soon as divided, the North and South are enemies. Even, if an amicable adjustment of national interests could be produced,—which is a supposition verging upon the very borders of impossibility—peace could not long be preserved. Unpleasant recollections would be deepened into feelings of distrust, irritation would be changed to bitter enmity. Thousands of men, unworthy the likeness of humanity, would make it a business to stir up dissention, that they might reap a golden harvest, though steeped in blood. A civil or an international war between the North and South, would be conducted with a murderous strife. Even now, the feelings of the great body of the people on both sides, are far from being as friendly as they ought. The South will not easily forget the *cause* of the abolition excitement; and on the other side the treatment of some northern men in Tennessee, in Georgia, and elsewhere, has produced deep feelings in the public mind.

The South may be assured, that it is an entirely gratuitous suspicion, which supposes the North to

be unfriendly to her interests. The South may be
assured that the North rejoices in her prosperity.
The great interests of both, although not identical,
are reciprocal; and it is susceptible of proof, that
they are mutually dependent upon, and flourish by
the aid of each other. The North is engrossed in
active enterprize, to which her situation and her
industrious habits both impel her—and is too busy
about her own concerns, to devise schemes for
injuring the South; and if the latter would put her
heads and hands to the like active enterprize, she
would have less time, and less inclination, to indulge
in suspicion that the North was endeavouring to
cripple or undermine her prosperity.

I have no hesitation in repeating what has been
frequently said, that the North has no disposition
to do injustice to the South. But still, if the former
believe that justice requires freedom for the slave,
and the latter by the same term understand a right
to keep him in bondage, there is a radical difference
of opinion between them; and nothing but the
wisest deliberation, joined with forbearance and
Christian principle, and aided by God's mercy, can
ever settle the question in an amicable manner.

XIII. In closing this chapter, I will take the
liberty to state my views as an individual, respecting the result of this controversy. In view of the
circumstances and opinions of the age, affecting
slavery in the civilized world, there are evident
indications that it will be abolished. Do not at-

tribute this belief to the spirit of abolition. I do not even give this opinion as a northern man, actuated by feelings of opposition to the South. Many of my prejudices were softened and removed by an actual interview with slavery. I came from that interview, impressed with a conviction, that the slaves were better off than their forefathers ever were in Africa; better off, as a body, than they would be, if emancipated and turned loose upon southern society—and with the strongest conviction, that they were *in every respect an injury to their masters.*

But I came from that interview—opposed to slavery; because the spirit of the age in the middle of the nineteenth century demands that the *American* negro should be placed in a situation to cultivate his moral and intellectual being — because slavery is detrimental to the moral, civil, and physical interests of the master — and because it is *utterly opposed to the spirit of American liberty.* Were I in Europe I could defend slavery upon the broad principles of legal enactments, and the customs of all ages; but, as an honest man, I could not defend it, in the face of Jefferson's Declaration. American slavery—after all our protestations of freedom, and boast of *man's* equality—is gross inconsistency.

With these views, although from the relative situation and condition of the North it will doubtless have a powerful influence in producing this result (emancipation), I believe it would take place, were the free states blotted out of existence. The spirit of Christianity and of civilization is against it. The South will not always be able to withstand the light which is pouring all around her. She now laughs to scorn the incipient advances of the enemy; and, mighty in her opinion of right, defies its power; but she has not yet grappled the giant. She has closed her doors, and looks out from the window, in imagined safety; but she knows not the subtlety of the foe. He comes in every wind, lurks in every corner: he presents himself to the eye, the ear, to every avenue of the understanding. The attempt to arrest the course of public opinion, will be like rolling back the stone of Sysiphus. The impulse which has been given to the spirit of freedom across the Atlantic, by the example of our institutions, is now re-echoed upon our shores, and points directly to slavery. Its voice is louder and louder. Almost all Protestant and Catholic Europe is against it. And in Europe our great national charter is understood *to mean what it says.* And surely it is pardonable to believe there is an inconsistency in declaring all men to be born " free and equal," and keeping one-fifth of these free and equal born in hopeless bondage. Perhaps the inconsistency appears more glaring from the fact, that some of the greatest American statesmen have utterly condemned the practice. Europe knows what Thomas Jefferson and Henry Clay have said of slavery,—although slaveholders themselves. Yet it is possible the light from continental Europe might be shut out, were it not for England. England, our own father-land, which, as the home of literature, arts, and Christianity, the South venerates far more than the North, has set an example on this subject, on which the eyes of the world are turned with eager interest. The result of her measures for colonial emancipation is not yet sufficiently obvious to be judged with correctness.

Should that result be favourable, the example and the influence of that country, will have a prodigious effect upon slavery throughout the civilized world; and these United States will feel that effect in its mightiest power. As well might the South attempt to silence the roar of the Atlantic upon her shores as to escape its influence. If England, by emancipation in her colonies, should prove to the world, not only that negroes are human beings, but that they are capable of self control as a free community, and of high intellectual, and moral improvement—that they are more virtuous, more peaceable, more industrious as free hirelings; in a word, that they are worthy of the same rights and privileges as men of Saxon or Roman descent—and should make these facts a comment upon the Declaration of American Independence, that all men " are entitled to life, liberty, and the pursuit of happiness," would southern slavery long be able to withstand public opinion; not of the free states—not of England and her dependencies alone—but of the civilized world?

I confess the idea of such a result elevates my mind above all considerations affecting any section or any interest of my native country, and gives me a loftier tone of feeling as a well wisher to my species.

In answer to all this it may be said, that slavery is not incompatible with republicanism, and Greece and Rome may be cited in proof. I will offer two considerations touching this point, for the reflection of the reader.

First. Slavery in ancient times was not confined to a distinct race as with us, nor was the object then, as now, merely pecuniary advantage. War and conquest were then considered almost the only *ennobling* employments, and upon the conquest of a state, or the sacking of a city, the whole surviving population—patricians and peasants—were dragged away by the conquerors, to be exhibited as trophies of their valor. After the exhibition they were slain, or sold by the soldiers—being considered only worthy to be menials, for their want of spirit in being taken alive. " Come back *with* thy shield, or *on* thy shield"—the Spartan mother's injunction to her warrior son—is a true picture of the spirit of that age, in which physical power was more honoured than intellectual or moral.

The other consideration arises from the greater responsibility which we incur as moral agents. "Where much is given, much will be required." Upon republican Greece or Rome Christianity never dawned. They were swayed by mere worldly motives in all their individual and national acts; and the law to love their neighbours as themselves had never sounded in their ears. The stream cannot rise above its fountain; and their gods, the fabrication of their ancestors, were of like passions with themselves. One of the maxims to which, as nations and as men, they most rigidly adhered, was always to resent an insult; and it is evident that human nature grows no better by age; for, in defiance of the law of God, it is a standing maxim of the world at present.

In conclusion, I know not with what view the considerations offered in this chapter may be received; but to my own mind, the exhortation of the apostle to the Athenians is strikingly applicable to American slavery—" the times of this ignorance God winked at, but now commandeth all men every where to repent."

CHAPTER III.

TO THE FREE STATES.

I. Free and slave states diametrically opposed—what influence this should exert on the former—why oppose the spirit of abolition—how the South may be reached.

II. Why slaveholders should be judged charitably—and the subject investigated—northern ministers appealed to—northern men at the South—severe taskmasters—why.

III. Power of habit, the stronghold of slavery, influence of filial and venerable associations among slaveholders—opposed to unconditional emancipation—why.

IV. Universal conviction of the right of property.—Value of slaves.—Ignorance of northern men respecting slavery.

V. Condition of the slave—observations of the writer—house servants many advantages—field labourers—negro houses—bad—mode of feeding slaves—various resources among them—public opinion in favour of humanity—dress of slaves—personal treatment—mode of labour—general appearance and manners—many of them in places of trust—general views of the whites—influence of the age on the slave.

VI. Free blacks of the South—situation unfavourable to improvement—interesting exceptions.

VII. Condition of the free blacks at the North—anecdote—degraded—outcasts—vicious—neglected by the whites—deep-rooted prejudice against them—proofs—what justice requires of the free states.—North not guiltless respecting slavery—what atonement for her own wrongs.

VIII. South devoted to the Union.—Interference of the North, on the question of moral right—appeal to the free states—to the clergy—examine motives—forbearance recommended among equals—injurious effects of northern denunciation.—Example of the Saviour.

I speak as unto wise men, judge ye what I say.

I. In the discussion of the subject of slavery, now in agitation in our country, you cannot act at all, nor exert any influence without incurring great responsibility. Indeed it is probable, that the result, or final decision of the question, will take its character, in a great degree, from the manner in which you treat it. You need, therefore, scarcely to be informed that, upon your wisdom, and prudence, the future welfare and destiny of this great nation depends.

The writer, being one of your number by birth and education, may be presumed to know something of your habits of thinking—your prejudices and sectional views,—and will take the liberty to animadvert plainly on the position you occupy in relation to this controversy; and endeavour to assist your inquiries, in view of forming a right decision upon the subject.

And the first, perhaps the most important point about which you need to be admonished is, to divest yourself of sectional prejudice. You have much yet to learn as a community, in order to judge this subject, with respect to reciprocal right.

You are deeply prejudiced against slavery, and, as a very natural consequence, against slaveholders. Many of you are ready to prove, *as clear as demonstration*, that slaveholding in every case, in every degree, is grossly wrong, a violation of every sentiment of justice, a daring sin against Heaven. In defence of this opinion, you will quote the Bible,—appeal to the views of moral and political right in which you were educated, and your own freedom from the sin. The slaveholder will make exactly the same appeal on his side—quoting the Bible,—the views of right in which he was educated,—and his consistent practice as proof. In this state of the subject, all the deliberation, the forbearance, the wisdom which fallen man can command, will be required in the progress and settlement of this question.

And remember, you cannot even agitate this subject, to produce any effect on the South, without being the aggressors. The South solicits you to let her alone. She asks not your counsel respecting the possession or treatment of her slaves; she earnestly requests you not to intermeddle with her domestic institutions. She claims, and justly too, that this is a question to be decided by her own free will.

Many of you will plead perhaps that slavery is a moral evil, and therefore ought to be abandoned. Admitting this to be true, what practical effect ought it to produce among you? Are you thence authorized to undertake its abolition by force? Have you received a commission to vindicate the cause of moral right, from the only source whence such a commission could emanate—the fountain of truth and justice? would you not individually, and as a community, resist to the utmost, every interference which assumed a right to *dictate* respecting the moral tendency of your own actions? The answer is too plain to admit a doubt.

Every question involving moral obligation, except so far as it affects the peace of society, is purely between man and his Maker. Of course when men design to exert an influence upon others, touching such questions, no weapons are allowable but those of a moral kind. This truth is too obvious to admit any doubt: and the people of the North have practised it with great effect on a subject deeply affecting the temporal as well as moral interest of society. I mean the subject of temperance.

Had the first agitators of temperance reform gone forth and taken the drunkard by the throat, and commanded him to abstain from his cups, because he was ruining himself; what would have been the result? Would not the universal opinion of society have condemned such measures? and would it not have increased rather than diminished the evil? What would be the effect, if ministers of the gospel should leave their appropriate sphere of "*persuading* men to be reconciled to God," and, by anathemas and violence, *compel* them to be pious? How soon would the pagan world be converted, if the missionaries sent to them should undertake to coerce their abandonment of heathenish idolatry?

But you do not harbour the idea of attempting to put down slavery by force; I am fully persuaded your views on this subject, as a question of moral right, are correct; but there is great danger, that, although you would not raise an arm to free the slave, the tendency of your measures will lead to the same result. If you, by persisting in a course of opposition to the known will and wishes of the South—by reproaches, threats, and criminations—produce an excitement leading to a civil or a servile war, will you not be answerable for the consequences, to God and man? The effect will be the same as if you marched an army to put down slavery. With this view of the subject, I call on you, as a sober, reflecting people, to oppose the *temper* of the immediate abolitionists. Whatever may be their principles, their *tone* and *manner* are at war alike with religion, and reason, and common sense. The spirit manifested in their publications, and many of their public resolutions, cannot be a good one. It is the spirit of denunciation, and curses, and vengeance. It reveals itself in reproaches, in bitter taunts, in indiscriminate invective. It does not breathe benevolence and good will to men, but exactly the reverse. It is the spirit of the worst persecution, for it bitterly denounces every thing that does not immediately bow to its own assumptions. I hazard nothing in asserting, that as soon as the *tone* of the immediate abolitionists becomes the standard of northern feeling on the question of slavery, there is an immediate end of this Union. The South would break the bond of union at a blow, without taking time to reflect upon the consequences.

But the South rejects your reasoning on this subject altogether. She denies the premises, and rejects the deductions. Probably a majority of the religious and moral part of the southern community will contend that slavery is morally right, and of the still larger class who profess no religion, and are not governed by moral motives, it is sufficient to secure their adherence to the practice even unto death, that it is for their interest. Now, whether right or wrong, you must first remove slaveholders from the ground they at present occupy as moral and thinking beings, before you can effect abolition. You must convince the man who admits his moral accountability, that slavery is sin; you must convince the man governed by wordly motives, that slavery is against his interest, and then you may make an impression upon the system.

To effect these objects, it is evident there is a large field to be explored. Every thing relating to slavery, as an institution or usage of society, is of importance in examining the subject. Neither individuals nor communities are ready at once, nor even immediately after full conviction of its injurious tendency, to renounce a practice which they have long cherished. There can be no doubt that the result of abolition movements upon the South, thus far, has been to withdraw the minds of slaveholders from all investigation of its moral and political bearing, and make them adhere to and support it more strenuously in self-defence.

II. I shall now endeavour to make such statements with regard to slavery, as some observation of its practical operation and effect upon society suggested, with a view of adding something to your knowledge of the subject, and enabling you to form a correct opinion of its merits.

First, I purpose to offer some observations on the situation and views of the whites or masters; which will lead us to contemplate the system in the light of cause and effect.

And the first reflection which strikes the mind, in taking a comprehensive view of the subject, is one of a moral nature. In condemning slavery, we unchristianize the South. The slave states, like the free, are divided into a great number of religious sects. These all, as a body, ministers and laymen, are slaveholders. Her presbyteries, associations, convocations, and conferences, all recognize its lawfulness—all participate in it—all repel charges brought against it. Surely this fact, although no justification of slavery, should, at least, influence us to be deliberate and cautious in condemning it in a wholesale manner. Were the practice sustained by one or two sects, and rejected by the others, there would be more ground for suspicion; but there are multitudes of ministers of each of the great denominations at the South, who have no more conscientious scruples in holding their slaves, than they have in preaching sermons. Are you ready, at your distance, to denounce a whole Christian community for holding to a practice which you consider unlawful? Until you have their views explicitly unfolded, and can comprehend all the circumstances which have a bearing upon the subject, charity should admonish you, not to be hasty in judging.

Either slavery is right, or these Christians are blinded to the truth; for it cannot be a moment believed, that they are all hypocrites, openly avowing and defending a practice which they know to be wrong. The question whether they are right should certainly be investigated, before they are summarily condemned; and even if they are proved to be wrong, passionate or harsh denunciation will have but little effect in opening their blind eyes, or in stopping their deaf ears. That they are not sinners " above all others" with regard to the deportment and character which should adorn the Christian profession, any one may judge for himself, if he will seek an interview. A minister in Virginia told me, that rum-selling and visiting horse races (a favourite amusement at the South,) he considered subjects of church discipline, and in his own church would not be tolerated. This minister was a slaveholder. Perhaps some of my readers may be inclined to class him with those who "strain at a gnat and swallow a camel." And here I will remark, that I *believe*, the ministry at the North generally, to say the least, are becoming more and more opposed to slavery. I have no reason to question their motives in this; but I must be permitted to enter a solemn protest against their summary denunciation of the practice, from conclusions formed in their own studies. If they heartily believe that it is a crying national sin, one upon which the judgments of Heaven are impending, they ought first to satisfy themselves of its enormity; and, if possible, go and view the offence and the offenders face to face, that they may be able to preach understandingly against it, and enforce their arguments by facts and illustrations drawn from their own observations. The ministers of the South do not act in a corner, nor would they be reluctant to meet a candid opponent in argument, or to hear all his candid objections against it. But a continual warfare and angry discussion at a distance, is contrary to the spirit of Christian benevolence, and to the first principles of justice. It produces continual irritation, and deepens prejudices which otherwise might be easily effaced. Even St. Paul did not thus act in his intercourse with the heathen world. The town-clerk of Ephesus exonerated him from the charge of blaspheming the goddess of the Ephesians. With a profound knowledge of human character, he judged that clamorous denunciations of their abominable idolatries would fill the popular mind with phrenzy or prejudice, and thus effectually exclude the doctrines which he designed to inculcate for their good.

And there is another observation to be made here, to which the candid attention of northern ministers is invited, while reflecting upon this subject. A great many ministers have gone from the free states as missionaries, teachers, and residents of the South. They had the fellowship and confidence of their brethren when they left, as pious, devoted men. Now what is the result? In a majority of instances, have they converted the slaveholders, or have the slaveholders converted them? Have they fallen into the errors of the community around them, or, like Noah, walked with God, while all others apostatized from him? Surely this fact of the general adoption of the practice of slavery by Christian men from the free states, should at least give some room for charity in judging it. And it is a source of complacency to the South, and not very creditable to the northern denunciators of slavery, that northern men, upon becoming residents of a slave state, very generally become slaveholders; and it is a notorious fact, that they are frequently the severest masters.

It is a common remark at the South, that the negro, when elevated to be an overseer, is the hardest taskmaster over his fellow-slave, and the slaveholder from the free states is the next. The reason of this severity, in the case of the latter, is easily explained; although the explanation will add more credit to northern character for enterprise and energy, than for clemency and humanity. The northern man is accustomed to a degree of activity, energy, and skill among mechanics and labourers, to which slaves are utter strangers. Consequently, he becomes impatient at their indolence and carelessness, and will very probably endeavour to hasten their operations by compulsion. Among native slaveholders, the master has been so long accustomed to the sluggishness of the negro, or rather has been accustomed to no other mode of labour, that it excites no surprise or impatience. After a sufficient experiment, the northern man, weary of exerting himself in vain to make the negro energetic and quick, gives up the point, by falling into the custom of his neighbours, and letting the slave pursue his own mode and system.

III. 2. The power of habit is perhaps nowhere more strikingly manifest than in the practice of southern slavery. The influence of this principle is here observed, as having the same control over a community that an inveterate habit has over an individual. No person can have an adequate idea of this fact, without actual residence among them. Slavery is a mere *matter of course.* To agitate the question of general emancipation in any form, would strike the community at large like proposing to them to give up their homes. The first question would be in either case, " how could we live without them ?" The practice has been so long continued, handed down from father to son, that it has become *necessary* to the present organization of society. The system is so interwoven with every fibre of society, that, to think of abandoning it, would seem like rending the different members of the body asunder. It has thrown a chain round society almost as difficult to cast off, as that which distinguishes *castes* in India. The inhabitants live as their fathers did, for they know no other way. Those people of the North, who see comparatively very few blacks, have very little idea of the construction of society at the South. Were some of them who associate every thing offensive with the idea of coming in contact with a negro, to see the order of things, where one half the society are blacks, they would soon learn there are more things on earth—

"Than are dream't of in their philosophy,"

and would obtain some new ideas of human character. It is mutually understood, both by master and slave, that the former is to do the *head* work, and the latter the *hand* work. And although this is a distinctive characteristic, yet as the direction of labour must constantly attend its operations, it brings the two parties into familiar contact, though entirely distinct. In the towns, and among the large planters, the slaves do all the labour, and perform all the menial services. As a general fact, a white man can do nothing even for himself personally, which another can do for him. In the house and abroad, a servant is in attendance. The parlour, the dressing-room, as well as the kitchen, are full of them. They come in contact with the family and guests at every corner. Hence there are various grades, and various duties assigned to each. A stranger to the system, closely observing the movements of the parties, would very soon see the effect of slavery upon the domestic organization of society.

Again, in another respect, the system of slavery possesses a very powerful influence upon the feelings of the community. It has been so long adopted and uncensured, been transmitted from father to son for generations, that it is associated with every thing venerable and filial. There is not perhaps a stronger or more deeply cherished feeling in the human breast, than respect and veneration for our fathers. And this feeling has a great influence when applied to the subject under consideration. "Surely a system which our forefathers approved and practised—a state of society in which they lived and died—cannot be wrong. The right to an inheritance, which was bequeathed to us by them, and transmitted to us by their last solemn act and testament; sanctioned by the laws of the land, and by the usages of the whole community, cannot be questioned." Thus the slaveholder reasons, for he is bred in the same undoubted right to the slave, that he is to the family mansion. The wealth of the father purchased both; his care and affection preserved them for his children. Is it strange, then, if under such circumstances, the son should not join the immediate abolitionists in denouncing his father's memory, and proclaiming to the world that his ancestors were all guilty of a most hateful crime. Their filial respect and gratitude are now indissolubly connected with their interests, and, with their present views and feelings, they would sooner perish on the tombs of their fathers, than do a deed which, in their opinion, would dishonour them. It requires but a limited knowledge of human nature, to judge of the powerful influence which such reasoning possesses over the minds of persons in their circumstances; and although the opposer of slavery will not admit its weight as an argument, it is a strong hold, which men of the world will hardly yield.

3. There is another objection, arising in the minds of slaveholders, when thinking seriously of emancipation, at which they revolt. It is the idea of having the slaves set at liberty, and yet remain in the community. *There must be a complete change in their views and feelings before they will consent to this.* There are many reasons which influence their minds, in utterly rejecting this proposition. A very strong one is the fact that the few free negroes, now living among them, are a miserable, idle class, outcasts of society, and looked upon with universal suspicion by the whites. So strong is the prejudice against free blacks, that in some of the states there are laws against any being made free, unless they are sent out of the state. Again, there is no doubt, in many instances, a feeling of proud superiority, which would not, for a moment, brook the idea of having the slave released from his condition of servility and dependence, and made in any respect an equal! There is also a very large class who would not be able to endure the thought of living without the continual services of the negro, so entirely dependent has habit made them upon the eyes, ears, and hands of others, for the most simple personal services.

But the grand objection of the community (and it is probably nearly universal) is the belief, that the negroes, if made free, would be the pest of society, and live by plunder and mischief. Naturally indolent—almost forced, at present, to perform their slight work—without intelligence to direct their labours—without any property—in a state of utter destitution—they would continually prey upon the whites, and live uncontrolled. Many, no doubt, think the lives and property of the whites would be at their disposal, and some even declare that the latter would be obliged to abandon the country to them. This is a serious question, and demands deliberate attention. The South will never harbor the thought of emancipation in this mode, without a radical change in public sentiment. It is sufficient to remark, that the southern people are the only proper judges of the mode of emancipation; and that whatever individual or community proposes a plan for their adoption, it should be done in the tone and manner of friendly counsel, not in the spirit of compulsive denunciation.

IV. But perhaps the most prominent fact suggesting itself to the mind of the observer in the slave states, is the almost unanimous conviction of the right of property in the slave. However they may differ in other respects, the slaveholders, as a body, are generally agreed in this. Depend upon it, the South at present feels a consciousness of right on the main question at issue, which is very little understood at the North. There are indeed many in the frontier states, who are harboring conscientious scruples as to the moral lawfulness of slavery, who feel that it is burdensome and wasteful, and know that it rests like a mountain of lead upon the energies of the state; but still, even these are not ready to allow you to touch the right of property. On this point, I will relate a single fact, among many similar which might be given. I was introduced to a gentleman, one who is well known in his neighbourhood for piety and philanthropy, as a northern man. In the seclusion of the parlour, he opened to me his views fully, on the subject of slavery—commencing himself with the remark, " I hope you have come to show us some feasible plan of putting away slavery." He conversed freely and openly, respecting his own views, —the state of public sentiment—and the action of legislation on the subject: but when the thought of abolitionists entered his mind, (just such views of northern abolitionists prevail all over the South, indeed this is a very favourable specimen) his voice and manner changed in a moment. " You," said he, pointing his finger at me, " you, northern abolitionists, have put a stop to all our designs for the benefit of the slave." "Why," he exclaimed, " should they attempt to take away *my property*, I would take down my rifle there, and fight to the last breath." This same man told me he could not conscientiously *sell* his slaves, unless he knew they would be better off than with him, and I have abundant proof that he was an indulgent master.

The South feel at present on this subject precisely as the people of the free states would, if some power, which had no shadow of right to intermeddle, should agitate the question of taking away—" peaceably if we can, forcibly if we must," one half of their property, embracing that part of it which was most valuable and available.

Connected with this view of the subject is the value of the slave. At a very moderate estimate of the value of the slaves in the United States, as property, they are worth five hundred millions of dollars. To bring the question more within the range of practical calculation, it may be safely assumed, that the slaves are more valuable than the plantations, were both put into the market, and they are also more available property. With their present views, all this property would be lost by emancipation, and their estates be without value. Have they not some reason to require, that if you wish them to give up their slaves—their means of living—leaving them entirely helpless—you should make them remuneration?

Thus I have endeavoured candidly to state some of the views of the South with regard to slavery, in reference to emancipation. That the reasons given operate with the weight of conclusive evidence in favour of slavery, need not be questioned. Whatever may be the impression among the people of the North, respecting the cogency of these reasons, they may at least learn what obstacles are to be removed before peaceable emancipation can be effected. *Those who consider slavery as a mere appendage to southern society, which may be thrown off with the same facility as an extra garment from an individual—are egregiously mistaken, and *know nothing about it.* It is emphatically an integral part of society itself, and its removal would produce a different organization or order. There is another class—perhaps wiser men—at the North, who would be willingly considered profound thinkers, and deeply read in the knowledge of human character and institutions, who do not see any very terrible consequences, in overthrowing the system at once, in the very face of all these obstacles. They look upon these objections, which I have briefly considered, only as so many deep-rooted prejudices, or more properly bug-bears, having no existence but in the imagination of the slaveholders. Like a man who has got an idea that there is a tremendous precipice in the path just before him, how cautiously and fearfully will he grope his way, and shrink back, involuntarily, at the thought of another step being his last. But when he has passed the utmost limits of the supposed danger, he will look back with surprise and chagrin, at the mighty fears his imagination had created. This is, indeed, a very pretty supposition, and all that these deep thinkers have to do is to get the slaveholders safe beyond the verge of the precipice.

V. What are the views and practices of the slaveholder, simply as a master, possessing, governing, and directing the slave, may perhaps be understood by considering

Secondly, The condition and treatment of the slave.

My own observations will form the basis of my remarks on this subject. I shall state what I have seen rather than what I have heard.

Upon entering a slave community for the first time, after thirty years' residence in the free states, my closest observation was directed to the condition and appearance of the blacks. I went with the feelings of a northern man—a liberal prejudice against slavery. My object was not to pry into secrets, and explore hidden mysteries,—not to hunt up isolated facts to use as arguments against slavery—not to note down trivial circumstances, to be expanded into marvelous narratives to feed insatiable appetites. I had a great curiosity to see a system or state of society, in my own country, about which I had heard and reflected so much. I wished to see it, and did see it, not in corners or in peculiar circumstances of great interest, but as an institution of society in its every day appearance. I had no interference with it—did not go out of my way to make discoveries—but made such use of my eyes, ears, and tongue, as inclination prompted.

Such is the foundation of the following remarks on the condition and treatment of slaves. I had no motive in seeing, which I would not willingly have made public—I have none in writing, but the well-being of my country. My first impressions of slavery were favourable. Candor obliges me to acknowledge that in no city of the North of the same class have I ever been, where the black population are so respectable in appearance—so well dressed—well behaved, and apparently so happy, as in the city of ——— where I first landed. I am also obliged to say, that this was the best specimen I saw in these respects,—of half a dozen cities and large towns I subsequently visited in that and the neighbouring states.

From what has been said of the familiar intercourse of household servants with their masters and families, it will of course be inferred that the former are expected and obliged to keep themselves very neat and respectable in their personal appearance, and habits, at least externally. And they exhibit a very distinct relationship to the human family of a lighter complexion, in their fondness for dress and finery. The most exquisite gentlemen in dress and politeness I ever saw, were blacks in a slave city. House and body servants frequently catch and copy the manners of their masters, so as to exhibit in their address, and in polite accomplishments, an exact imitation. You may observe two dandies pass in the street, and salute each other, and touch their hats with a grace which few white men ever attain.

From the circumstances of their situation, the

servants having close and constant intercourse with the family, have many privileges and advantages. Their burdens are not heavy, their labours far from being severe. They appear to enjoy life as well or better than any other class in the community; and when not actually employed, the streets and corners are loud with their gossip and laughter.

In descending to the country, slavery wears a different aspect. According to the circumstances and style of the master, a greater or less number of each sex are employed in the necessary services of the house, as in the large towns; the rest are field hands or outdoor labourers. It is an object for slaves to get a station about the house. The labour is lighter, and the fare better, and they are all very fond of the good things of the kitchen.

The field labourers live in huts by themselves, which, on small plantations, are generally built in the immediate vicinity of the family residence. These huts are called the *negro quarters*, and the impression they made on my mind was more unfavourable to the practice of slavery than any thing I saw. I hesitate not to say, they are too often alike unworthy the master and the slave. I doubt whether the cabins of the natives on the banks of the Gambia are so poor and miserable. I never entered one of them, but have looked into several, and seen numbers in traveling. They are constructed of plank or logs, or logs and clay, and are very generally in a dilapidated condition; and from the specimens I saw, with nothing worthy the name of furniture. The farmers' hovels or cattle sheds at the North, taking the average of both, are better buildings, except that the cabins are probably somewhat tighter. I regret to say these things—I say them in hope of producing reform.

There is a manifest pride in the master in having his slaves, particularly those about his house and person, in good condition; but to see a large mansion, a worthy residence for a governor, with its beautifully shaded inclosures and graveled walks, and tasteful gardens, flanked at a little distance in front by half a dozen wretched hovels, unfit to tenant any human beings, is a scene unworthy of old Virginia.

The slaves on small plantations, and with humane masters, are generally supplied with food from the household kitchen. A sufficient quantity is prepared at each meal for the whole establishment, and after the master and family have eaten, the remainder is carried out to the servants in their quarters, without measure or weight. This is the most favourable mode for the slave, as he has the same food as the master. But the general practice in feeding slaves is by rations—a given quantity to each person. The great staple is corn. This is measured so much to a person or family, for a given time, and prepared by themselves. I am unable to state to what extent meat rations are allowed. Some masters deny meat to slaves altogether, but I believe these are comparatively few. In a country where pork is plenty, and an article of universal consumption, the slaves are extensively furnished with it, and is generally given out to them, once a year, at the time of slaughtering, so much for an individual or family. Many of them also raise pigs and chickens, which they may consume or sell. And I believe it is a very general practice all over the South, to allow slaves patches of ground which they may appropriate as they please. They raise corn, cotton, tobacco, or vegetables, and sell them for their own profit. This kind of tithing, or allowing slaves a part for themselves, is observable also in other things. A negro brings a load of wood to market, and you will see several long sticks slung on the outside of his cart. He delivers you the load, and you question him about the outside sticks. " Dat *mine*, massa, I get quarter dollar for dat." You buy it of course.

There is also a great variety of wild fruits, increasing as you proceed South—to which the negroes have access. On large estates, and where the "force" is under the control of a hard-hearted and selfish manager or overseer, I have no doubt there are instances of deprivation and actual suffering. But the reader may be assured the negroes perfectly understand the first law of nature—self support. If sufficient is not given them, they have little difficulty in helping themselves. They gather the crops, do all the work, and every thing that is their master's passes through their hands. The right is theirs, the moon and stars their friends; and dogs, bolts, and bars are insufficient to keep them from providing for themselves in case of necessity. They have also some resources, which avail them more or less. One is grumbling. They are inveterate grumblers when they are not suited. I have seen a slave tell a white man, who threatened to give him no dinner,—very respectfully of course—that " he could not work without he had enough to eat," and I have little doubt that if the slave was cut off from his dinner, the master was cut short in his work. If the slave has not enough to eat, he will obstinately neglect or spoil his work Experience has taught masters that it is for their interest to have servants well fed, well clothed, and well treated.

I am unwilling to believe the southern slave, except in rare instances, suffers for want of food. There are here, as everywhere else—brutes in human form—men who fear not God nor regard man. An example was mentioned of a man, in Maryland, who possessed several hundred slaves, and from whose manner of feeding them, both as to quality and quantity, humanity revolts. " What do his neighbours say about him?" I inquired. " What do his neighbours say about him," repeated my informant, (a slaveholder himself,)—" what *don't* they say about him." There is public opinion in favour of humanity at the South; and the man who sets public opinion at defiance among slaveholders, is estimated in society there as he is everywhere else.

The slaves are habituated to rise very early in the morning and commence their labours, and, so far as I have observed, quit their work at supper or sunset, and then they are free till the next morning. It is not customary to require services of field labourers after night fall, except on extra occasions, although, at such times, I have no doubt, unreasonable services are sometimes required of them.

With regard to dress, the slaves are generally comfortably supplied. Their clothing is strong and coarse, but whole and decent. In many instances in the country, the master and servant are clothed from the same piece. And yet there are some so patched, like Joseph's coat, with many colours, that it would puzzle even Yankee ingenuity to discover the original cloth. I have seen some suits, which must have represented all the garments used in the family mansion since the revolution. The common clothing is supplied by the master, of course—generally in the same mode as rations —so many garments and pairs of shoes per year; but whenever a holiday suit is required, the slaves, unless lucky enough to obtain the cast off garments of the family, supply themselves. I believe most slaves of both sexes have suits better than their every day clothing, and the fact is creditable to the master and servant. The avails of their gardens, and the means obtained for little services, from guests of the family and others, are expended for this purpose. Servants in large towns and vicinities obtain considerable money in this way, which is considered their own. And probably not a few purloin and sell the property of their masters, and apply the avails to their own use.

The main question will here be asked, what is the personal treatment of the slave? It is a point which should be satisfactorily settled if possible, for there is a great prejudice against slavery in some sections, on account of real or supposed inhumanity to the negro. And there are some very compassionate people who believe the master is engaged, a considerable part of his time, with a terrible cat-o'-nine tails, and who think the lash is continually resounding from the Delaware to the Sabine. I am by no means prepared to answer this question, from extensive observation; for during a year a half contact with slavery, I have never seen a slave flogged or sold. Doubtless I might, had I been ambitious of looking up such spectacles, but in "minding my own business," no such remarkable occurrence has fallen under my notice. I will endeavour, however, to throw some light on the subject, and at least put the reader in the way of answering the question for himself.

And the first suggestion I would offer is this, how do the people of the free states treat their servants, and how would they treat them, were they in the bondage of southern negroes? The northern reader can immediately refer his thoughts to certain persons of his acquaintance who would be cruel masters, but of the great body of his neighbours he has a better opinion. Human nature is radically the same every where. The North will perhaps lay claim to more religion, purer morals, and a higher philanthropy to soften their dispositions; and so far as this is the fact allowance is to be made,—otherwise they may judge very exactly of the treatment of southern slaves, by the mirrors in their own bosoms.

The slave is taught from childhood that his business is to labour, and he goes to his snail-pace employment as a matter of course. On large plantations there are overseers to direct the labourers and keep them at work. If the slave should be refractory or disobedient, he would be subdued in a summary manner. If, in the absence of the master or overseer, he should not perform a reasonable amount of labour, he would very probably suffer some punishment, — most likely corporal chastisement—and certainly for a repetition of neglect. That the master or manager follows him into the field, and urges him forward with a whip, is, I am persuaded, but a rare occurrence; and that the slaves, as a body, are not goaded and driven in their tasks, I am satisfied from two considerations.

First,—public sentiment is against it. There is, as I have before stated, a kind of tacit agreement between the master and slave, that the latter should take his own course as to activity of muscular motion, provided he keeps regularly at work; and out of his accustomed track he cannot be driven with impunity or safety. About a certain amount of positive labour is expected of each hand, according to his ability. This certain amount is pretty definitely understood by both parties, and does not exceed half of what is performed by a northern labourer. The master who should persist in forcing his hands to much greater exertion, would generally find himself in difficulty. His work would be neglected or spoiled—his slaves would run away, if they did nothing worse—he would be marked by the community as an inhuman master, and hated by his own subjects. It is impossible to keep slaves from communicating with each other; what is done on one estate is known through the neighbourhood.

Secondly,—there is *prima facie* evidence of the general freedom of the slave from great severity of treatment, which to my own mind is of great weight. I was greatly disappointed at the general appearance and manners of this class of society. As a body they are erect in posture, with manly figures, personally in good condition or well fed, and with a boldness of look, not found among human beings, either burdened with guilt or ground to the dust by an iron rigour. A slave will look a white man in the face with as much confidence, and as little wavering of the eye, as one of his equals. There is an air of servility about them in all their communications with the whites, as a matter of course—a negro is taught to touch his hat to a white man as a superior; he does it almost mechanically—but there is very little abjectness of demeanor. I have been often struck with these facts in my observation of slavery, and they afford conclusive evidence that the negro has not lost all sense of manliness in his bondage. There is a large number among them who appear almost to have lost the idea of slavery. Many of them have the management of farms at a distance from their masters, with a sufficient force to perform the labour. I have had acquaintance with some such, who for that information most useful to farmers, such as is derived from experience and observation, are equal to white men — perhaps superior; for being ignorant of letters, their mental capacities are all centered in observing the operations of nature, and the practices of other men—while for shrewdness and manliness in managing bargains, they are not a whit behind their masters. Many are teamsters or wagoners, who are intrusted with loads of produce to carry to market,—sometimes on journeys of hundreds of miles; and carry back merchandize for the country merchants. Others are mechanics, millers, or coachmen, all of whom are men in manners, deportment, and sagacity, far above the degree which ignorance of practical slavery has assigned to such a state. I believe the idea of degradation dwells much more strongly in the breast of the master than the slave. Some of the former, at least in sentiment, profess to hold the latter as an inferior to the last degree. A white man—(and a Christian man if profession makes a Christian), said, " I will lose the last drop of my blood before I will be insulted by a negro," although the insult in this instance consisted in the slave refusing to do what he was ordered, having received a contrary order from another, who had at least an equal right to his services. Of course this Christian man was in a tremendous passion.

There is a very general belief throughout the South, that the negro requires a chastisement occasionally; a sort of periodical flogging, to keep him obedient and respectful—otherwise he would become impudent, insolent, and intolerable. I am not sufficiently acquainted with slavery in detail, to judge the correctness of this common, almost universal, sentiment; nor whether the practice of the master accords with his belief. But I have heard the remark from persons living in the slave states, and who were *opposed to slavery from principle*, giving, as a strong feature of the negro's character, an inclination to be impudent and insolent.

But one fact is very evident; they are very much inclined to scold, and fret, and quarrel among themselves, especially females, and require a firm voice and steady hand to keep them from uproar, or injuring one another. It is a curious fact, that the last epithet of reproach which they can use in anger, is to call each other *negro*. If ordered by one of their own colour to do any thing to which they have a disinclination, the scornful answer is, "I don't do nigger's work."

In summing up the particulars mentioned on this subject, I am ready to conclude that, in the physical treatment of southern slaves, they are better off than their fellows of any other age or country. In view of the fearful power of the master to possess, work, punish, or sell the slave almost beyond responsibility; and in view of the disposition of men to exceed the bounds of justice or moderation where they have power, it must be conceded the southern slave has a very tolerable lot; and his condition must of necessity grow better or worse. He cannot stand still while the world is advancing around him. The increasing light must be hidden from him, or it will have a decided influence upon him. Though at an almost immeasurable distance, he follows in the footsteps of his master. Although his fellow man has denied him the use of letters, he cannot deprive him of those avenues to the mind with which God has endowed him. The negro sees the triumph of art in the steamboat and rail-road, and he feels a degree of the enthusiasm of his master. He even feels a pride of country in these achievements of art. His constant intercourse with his white superiors has imparted a portion of their intelligence to him. He reflects and reasons, although in a limited sphere, and associates the ideas of freedom and wealth with all the improvements around him. To be sure, habit and hereditary degradation have destined him to a life of servility. Every thing about him—all his senses—combine to teach him that his master is strong, and he weak; the one rich, the other poor. But the advancement of society will find him a willing disciple, and an apt scholar; and when the amount of knowledge among slaves shall be sufficient for them to exert an influence upon each other, and thus impart intelligence among themselves, faster than that received by reflection from the master, as at present, the relative position of the community will soon be very different. The influence or result of that change, time only can determine.

VI. I will here make a few remarks on the free blacks of the South. *As a class*, they are in a worse condition than the slaves. They have little more intelligence, and are more out of the way of acquiring information, being at a greater distance, and having less intercourse with the whites. They look upon the slaves as being obliged to work, and they exhibit positive evidence of being free from the obligation by their idleness. It is also a very general belief that they get their living mostly by stealing. They are not so well clothed, and less respectable in appearance and manners, than the slaves. They are also a source of continual suspicion, and their situation seems to be in every respect unpleasant and unfavourable to improvement.

But to these general remarks there is an interesting exception. In all the cities of the South, there is a class of free blacks who have risen above all the obstacles that surround them, and, by perseverance in well doing, have established a character for honesty and industry, and are in prosperous circumstances. They are barbers, mechanics, porters, hackmen, and, especially, waiters. This last appears to be the most suitable employment for the negro. It is a situation which seems to be adapted to his taste and genius, and he takes pride in showing his capability in it. Experience makes him an adept in all its details. It is here, if anywhere, his activity and energy are brought to light. And from the acknowledged worthlessness of the great body of servants, those in whom confidence can be placed are always in demand, and obtain good wages.

VII. As a suitable conclusion to this part of the subject, I purpose to offer a few remarks on the condition of the blacks in the free states. In doing this, I shall avoid all extended comparisons. It has required some exertion of the will throughout this work to keep my pen from instituting comparisons between the North and South, while treating of slavery. Many might be made highly illustrative of sectional characteristics, but I am aware they might seem invidious to certain classes of persons, and would perhaps have a tendency to deepen that feeling of prejudice (already sufficiently watchful), which it should be the aim of every person, whose object is the dissemination of truth and justice, to allay.

This would be a suitable place for treating upon the capacity and character of the African, but the discussion of that subject does not fall within the limits of this work. I will venture, however, to remark, that, in the present condition of the negro, the community will never agree respecting it. Reflections will naturally arise in the minds of the inquisitive, but it would be altogether unjust to judge of what he is capable of attaining, as an intellectual being, from his present state. It is an undeniable fact, that, *throughout this Union*, he is considered and treated as a degraded inferior. When we reflect upon the slow progress made even by our English forefathers, in the arts of life and mental cultivation for three hundred years past, at which period the mass of the people were probably behind the present American negroes, we can form some opinion of the length of time the latter would require, in the most favourable circumstances, before it would be fair to decide upon his capacity. That he partakes in an eminent degree of the indolence and the propensity for animal indulgence, so conspicuous in the natives of warm climates, cannot be questioned; whether they are increased or diminished by his condition of slavery, it is difficult to determine. That he is the subject of strong passions, both fierce and gentle, must be evident to every one who has made any observation on his character. The following anecdote has often occurred to me in observing the condition of the African race, as illustrative of its degraded, unsocial state in this country. I was acquainted with a very respectable coloured shoemaker, while a resident of one of the northern cities, a few years ago, whom I sometimes employed in his occupation. I frequently entered into conversation with him, and, observing several white men in his employ, endeavoured to excite in him a feeling of sympathy in favour of his race.

I immediately discovered that the subject was one on which he had been thoughtful. "Sir," said he, suspending his work, and looking me in the face, "I have tried to do them good, but I can't. They won't learn. I have had a dozen coloured apprentices, and they every one left me after staying one, two, or four months. They were never used to any work, and it was so irksome to be confined to it, they had rather run away, and live by begging and stealing. Not one in twenty will make a man good for any regular business. It is the fault of their parents."

Every northern man can judge how far this statement of the coloured shoemaker is a fair representation of the character of the blacks of his acquaintance.

Now permit me to ask you, citizens of the free states, what is the moral and physical condition of your black population? Are you authorized, in view of a comparison between them and the southern slave, to throw the first stone? The fathers of these blacks were slaves. In your wisdom, you gave them prospective freedom. Their emancipation is now nearly complete. What improvement have they made as a community, and what influence have you exerted on them, and they on you? Again; with a knowledge of their habits and character would you be willing to have a black population, as numerous as that at the South, added to your own? If I mistake not, the condition of the blacks among you, does not reflect much credit upon your philanthropy. You hate slavery. I fear you also hate the negro. Certainly there is a great lack of evidence that you regard his welfare. Your blacks are in many respects in a worse condition than those in the South. They are actually, as a body, more out of the way of improvement. You have no immediate intercourse with them. You hold them at a great distance. Generally ignorant, suffering under the ban of a *felt* neglect and degradation, their liberty seems to be comprized in a freedom to commit vice. In a civilized and Christian community, they receive scarcely any of its benefits. True, many of them in the large towns are respectable waiters, barbers, and kitchen servants, but in the country, and the vicinity of your villages, the negroes are scattered in rude huts—perhaps a little better than those mentioned in Virginia—at a distance from other habitations, and live precariously by day's work and pilfering. The farmers generally reject their services, because there is no dependence upon them. They almost universally drink to excess, and are otherwise in gross debasement. The churches and public schools are indeed open to them, but it requires a degree of hardihood but few persons in their circumstances possess to avail themselves of these privileges. Do the ministers look them up, like stray sheep, and invite them to the sanctuary? Do the teachers encourage them to attend school; and if any of them come, do they take an interest in their instruction, or turn them off, with such attention as is "good enough for negroes?" Do the community, as a body, exhort, encourage, and strive to lead them in the ways of well doing, or do they, by their neglect and reproaches, pronounce them out of the pale of decency and respectability? In proof that the above is the character and condition of your black population, I appeal to the calendars of your courts, and the records of your jails and penitentiaries. Examine these, and see what proportion the convictions for murder and penitentiary crimes bear to the relative population of white and black. If there is great disparity against the latter, the cause must be found, either in a more vicious disposition, or in the unfavourable circumstance of his situation. I leave you to the choice of the dilemma.

It appears to me evident, that there is deep, unmitigated prejudice against the negro. His condition and situation in the free states proclaim this. In how many of these states can he be a legal freeman or voter, let his property or respectability be what they will? Legislative acts, and the popular voice also, proclaim this. I will instance only one fact, the result of the Canterbury School in Connecticut. Public opinion was very deliberately brought to bear on that question, and the consequence was, a judgment of the highest court— sustained by the public, and more recently sanctioned by legislative enactments, in the little but enlightened state of Connecticut, that the negro was not a *citizen*, in the high and proper sense of the term—but a being inferior to the white man. Now it appears to me evident that justice requires the free states to improve the condition of their blacks, before they take any urgent steps for the emancipation of the southern slave. The South might now very justly say to them, if you have so great a regard for the negro, begin at home; educate and elevate your own, make them good citizens, honest and intelligent, and then you may hold them up to the view of the world, as examples of the capability and worth of the negro among a community of whites. At present, we can see no improvement in the African by emancipation, *from your example*. At least, let us have a plain example to follow, before we are called upon to give up our inheritance.

I have stated my conviction in a former chapter, that slavery is destined to come to an end. But there is no good foundation for the belief that emancipation will be sudden or immediate. And whenever the period arrives, the work must be accomplished either by the free action of the slave states, or a civil convulsion. Suppose for a moment, the righteous judgment of Heaven should permit the latter, what reason have you to offer why you should not suffer your full share of the calamity? In a moral point of view, the North, or free states, are not guiltless in this matter. They have another burden to be removed, besides the sin of being part of a slave nation. Northern cupidity carried slaves from Africa, and sold them to the South. And there are plenty of merchants and sailors among you who would do it now, were it not unlawful. Some of the most costly mansions in New England were built with the profits of this traffic, and still stand as monuments of its greatness. Why not go to the owners of this property, and bid them sell it, and give the money to benevolent objects, as, in some measure, an atonement for the guilt. In some instances the lineal descendants of the slave dealer occupy the premises, just as the sons of the original purchasers possess the southern slave.

Some of you have heard from the lips of the old negro, by the youthful fireside, the story of his being ambushed and stolen by the white man, while playing with his mates among the palms of his native Guinea. Could the cry of Africa for retribution be heard by mortal ears, it would fall with appalling sound upon the Christian land of New England and the free states. What have they done to atone for these forgotten wrongs?

Has emancipation done it? It does not acquit the robber or assassin, to promise he will not repeat the crime. Paying a thousand new debts will never cancel an old one. After serving yourselves as long as you thought prudent with these slaves, you turned them loose upon the wide world, poor, ignorant, friendless, without even a "God bless you" to cheer their lot; and now you spurn and reproach, and heap indignity upon them, because they do not in a moment rise up miraculously your equals. Oh, the heart that kindles in commiseration of human suffering is ready to wish these injured outcasts might borrow the jewels of gold, and jewels of silver, and precious things of their neighbours, like their fellow bondmen of old, and like them escape in their father-land, to enjoy, with God's blessing, the reward of their fathers' labours in peace.

Or, what will you gain, morally or physically, from the result of this fearful struggle? Suppose you demand emancipation. The South repels your demand as unjust, and dares you to the trial of right. Will you be more prosperous, or leave a better name, or better inheritance to your posterity, or rejoice in emancipation, after the work is accomplished by violence. Will you rejoice in the ruins of a country—of a nation of brothers, which your own doings have investigated? I have thus imagined a scene, which may Heaven never suffer to be realized. It is indeed not beyond the limits of human folly, but there is great reason to hope that forbearance and justice will prevail, and this fair and glorious inheritance of ours will be spared the horrors of a civil or a servile war.

Let the North be assured that the South is not a whit behind her in patriotic devotion to this Union. The South loves the Union, and is willing to make important sacrifices for its preservation. Through the Revolution, and in all the national struggles since, she has borne a conspicuous part. In this controversy, she asks, as a question of simple justice and legal right, for the same quiet possession of her domestic policy that you enjoy in yours. She asks it as a right conferred on her by the confederation of the states. So far from being an infraction of the Constitution, she claims that it distinctly recognizes slavery. And she will charge you with the consequences of breaking your solemn obligations, in sealing that instrument, if you offer such an interference with her rights, as will lead to a dissolution of the Union.

But you claim to be actuated by higher motives than mere patriotism. You found your interference upon the question of moral right—the claims of eternal justice and truth. Exhibit your evidence that Heaven has delegated you to sit in judgment upon the moral conduct of your fellows, and every good man in the Union will rally to your standard. But your most distinguished writers on morals, explicitly deny that you have any right to offer coercive interference. Such a proceeding would inevitably make matters worse.

Rather than consent to this, I would say, leave slavery to the course of events ordained by Divine Providence. I do not ask you to abate your abhorrence of slavery. I know its strength. But I do ask you to ponder well the course of action you pursue: as has been said in appealing to the South, so I say to you, sacrifice even slavery to the Union. In view of present evil, or future retribution, there can be little hesitation in the bosom of a good man, in choosing whether to bear the sin of belonging to a slave nation, or of taking a part in forcibly overthrowing it. And I put this question distinctly to the clergy of the free states, a class of men whom I extensively know to be philanthropists and republicans; and generally worthy of the great influence they possess on questions of morals. In a community so intelligent, and moral, and religiously influenced as the North, the clergy will have to bear, in a great measure, the responsibility of the decision on this subject, whatever it may be.

Again. If you begin deliberately to inquire what you shall do to correct the wrong of slavery, first examine the heart—go down into its deepest recesses, and discover, if possible, the motives from which you are to act. The judgment is greatly liable to be prejudiced and influenced by early associations, and long-cherished opinions, and modes of thinking. What is your practice, or what agency do you exert in abolishing other evils? As Christians you are opposed to intemperance and pagan idolatry, as republicans to monarchy and tyranny. But you never seriously think of opposing these and other practices different from your own, with any other weapons than those of persuasion. Perhaps you will say, all these evils are foreign; whereas slavery is an evil in our own country, and among our own citizens. True, but for that very reason ought you to exercise greater forbearance and charity. These fellow-citizens enjoy the same rights, privileges, immunities, and blessings as yourselves. The liberty, civil and religious, which you enjoy, is a common inheritance, equally possessed, equally purchased. These citizens practise customs different from your own, and in your view incompatible with civil liberty and moral accountability. But is it not an unwarrantable assurance which arraigns them before the bar of your judgment. They acknowledge neither the crime nor the jurisdiction of the court. You send missionaries to convert the heathen, but you instruct them not to coerce, but to persuade and convince the gross idolater. Have you so little faith in the agency of these instruments in reclaiming your *equals*, that you resort to violence and denunciation?

If you discovered your brother in a place of danger of which he was unconscious, would you endeavour to show him his situation in a kind or a harsh manner? Would you burst forth in a torrent of reproach at his folly or want of foresight, in bringing himself into this danger; or would you propose some mode of relief or escape, in a spirit of brotherly affection and sympathy? Which does Christian and moral benevolence dictate? Which will have the most powerful influence, in view of the character of human nature? Have you followed the guidance of wisdom, and the "golden rules" in treating this subject? Instead of offering friendly assistance and persuasion, have you not oftener charged them as slaveholders, with the crime of living in known violation of the laws of God and man?—while a great majority of them, be assured, acknowledge no such crime. Instead of exhorting them to repentance, in the spirit and language of St. Paul, have you not frequently denounced against them the judgments of Heaven? Instead of offering to relieve them of a burden, you have heaped ridicule upon it.

And especially, will you denounce all slaveholders as on one common level? Will you, by your action and measures, force those back with the multitude, who are anxiously looking for some way of escape from their bondage? The reason that the South fling back every thing that comes from the North, is the fault of the latter. The spirit and language of the North, when speaking of slavery, has been without discrimination; harsh, bitter, reproachful. There are many exceptions, but this is the fact generally. Comparisons have been drawn unfavourable to the South, and touching them in very sensible points. Besides this, you make no allowance for the sanctions of time and custom; none for the peculiar circumstances, for the long-cherished feelings and habits of slaveholders. Believe it; there are many men, men of great respectability, south of the Potomac, who consider themselves in far greater, more distressing bondage, by the system of slavery, than their own slaves. I say this, from a firm conviction of its truth. There are others who are halting between two opinions. Now I verily believe that the tendency of northern action, and northern language, and northern feeling, is to drive these men back to a reconciliation with slavery, instead of offering them sympathy and aid in a manner which they can accept.

The modern improvements of the age in the arts of life have in themselves no power to make men radically better. Their aim is entirely superficial. They have no influence upon the heart, the seat of moral affections. Their tendency is to inflate little man with great pride. Luxury and effeminacy, vice and oppression, follow their footsteps with fearful certainty. Nothing but that spirit of benevolence which was manifested by Him, who, when he was reviled, reviled not again; whom the direst persecution could not swerve from pursuing the object of his mission into the world—unsought and unrequited goodwill to men: nothing but this spirit can save our country, or carry it safely through the agitation and distraction of this vexing, this momentous controversy.

CHAPTER IV.

TO THE UNION.

I. What can be done? Subject of vast magnitude—radical difference of opinion.

II. Three modes of settling the question stated.

III. Faint hope that either side will abandon its position—ultra slaveholders—violence of southern excitement a favourable omen—no prospect of the North becoming in favour of slavery—reasons—will not use force against it.

IV. Dissolution of the Union considered—its probable consequences and result.

V. Third mode of settling the question—by compromise and concession—why it may be hoped for—desirable that southern men should express their views—prevented by abolition movements.

VI. Colonization recommended—abolitionists opposed—mistaken philanthropy—colonization emancipation must become a national question. South will reject every other mode—urged from motives of regard for the welfare of the coloured race—negroes cannot rise to equality with the whites—proved in the free states—in Philadelphia—slaves to remain in the country as hired servants considered—South will oppose it, and why—no encouragement from the example of the North. British emancipation referred to—final consequences not known.

VII. Why the coloured man should go to Africa—climate considered—comparisons invited—America owes it to Africa to send back her children. God intends it by our prosperity—government must do it—influences of colonization on Africa. Question of expense alluded to—money lost in Florida war.

VIII. Some slave states have begun the work—reasons for government interference—partizan politics, the curse of our country—the only hope of benevolence in the future.

Liberty and union, now and forever, one and inseparable.

I. "WHAT can be done to settle the agitation on the great subject of slavery; and decide the controversy in an amicable manner, satisfactory to all parties; with reference to the claims of justice, and the best interests of humanity?" This question is often asked by men of inquisitive and reflecting minds; but in view of its vast magnitude, and the difficulties which seem to bar up every avenue of approach, human wisdom bows before it.

There is indeed no lack of propositions on the subject; but none has been offered which is not objectionable to large portions of the community. And while the suggestions of common minds are rejected as unequal to the exigency, men of wiser and more comprehensive judgment will cautiously deliberate before assenting to propositions, which, however plausible in theory, involve an unknown amount of experiment in the execution. It is not the welfare of an individual which is at stake, but a question respecting the rights and the well being of six or seven millions of fellow-men. In another view, the integrity of a nation, already one of the first rank—and destined, as far as human foresight can judge, to exceed all that have preceded it in intellectual and physical power, and promising by its youthful enterprise and intelligence to exert a powerful agency in the great drama of human affairs.

But the greatest obstacle to the settlement of this question, arises from the fact, that there is at present, beyond all controversy, a radical difference of opinion between the free and slave states on the subject. There are great classes on each side, whose views differ respecting various minor points; but as communities, they will unite on the great principles; the latter, that slavery in their circumstances is justifiable and lawful; and the former, that it is unlawful in all circumstances whatever. Admitting these views of the case to be correct (and I would gladly be convinced of error if wrong), there are but three modes of settling the question.

II. First. By one side giving up the principle.
Second. By a dissolution of the Union.
Thirdly. By mutual concession and compromise. The attention of the reader is directed to some remarks on each of these modes.

III. On the first, I purpose to be very brief, as the former chapters have anticipated the most prominent facts and reflections on this head.

With their present views, and in the position they now occupy with regard to each other, there is scarcely a ray of hope that either side will abandon the ground it has taken. From the unfavourable commencement of the controversy, the parties are not in a mood to look at the subject dispassionately. The consequence resulting from the agitation thus far, is a determination of each side to adhere to, and persist in, its sectional views with increased prejudice. Pushed but a little further, this result will eventuate in the direst national calamity.

With regard to the South, it is impossible to predict what influence may result from a more sober and conciliating tone, or a proposition to compromise, from the northern states; nor from the great experiments which are in progress in the British colonies; nor from the increasing light and improvements of the age; but *with their present views and feelings*, the South is ready to join issue with all the world on the main question—the right of slavery. Perhaps below the latitude of Tennessee, a great majority hold it with Governor McDuffie of South Carolina, who invoked Heaven that "his posterity, to the latest generation, might never live in any other state than one of domestic slavery." I never saw a northern man read this invocation without smiling. An honourable senator also from the same state, recently stated in Congress (in substance), that every abolitionist caught in that state should be hung, in defiance of all earthly power.

These statements from men who may be presumed to represent the popular will in their section—and as they have been corroborated by acts of violence farther south, give us pretty substantial evidence of public sentiment in the slave states. But, as an individual, I am ready to hazard a belief that the past violence of the South, in word and deed, is a favourable omen. The suddenness of southern excitement is a proof that it was not the result of deliberate reflection; and its violence shows that it has pre-occupied the public mind, and closed up every avenue to calm investigation. The South is, indeed, from its state of society, exposed to danger from the agency of incendiaries, but not to an extent which its vigilance and censorship of the periodical press would justify. These must be attributed, mainly, to the sudden and maddening effects of the unwarned, and ill-judged irruption of abolition philanthropy. But as the violence of the storm is soon wasted in proportion to its fury, so the ebullition of popular excitement prostrates the energies of public phrenzy, and leaves society better prepared for dispassionate and calm reflection. That this will be the result; that the South will ere long condescend to discuss the subject of slavery calmly, on the question of its merits, and with respect to its moral and political bearing upon society, there is great reason to hope; that this period will be hastened or retarded, as well as its ultimate effect influenced by the temper and action of the free states, cannot be doubted.

That the North will abandon its principles on this subject, there is no foundation for believing. Having deliberately given her own slaves freedom, it is to be presumed that she ardently wishes her example in this respect to be universally followed. It is in her view a question both of morals and of interest; and although the former doubtless greatly preponderates, yet, in both aspects, she views it as a question deeply affecting the welfare of the South, and affecting herself indirectly. Should the civilized world, as it advances in intelligence and in the progress of free discussion, speak in terms of reprehension of slavery, her voice would join that of universal public opinion, for this is now decidedly the sentiment of her people. She perhaps claims that her own freedom gives her an elevated standing, better suited to a deliberate view of the subject; but she may be assured that by obtaining her information at second hand, as the mass of society necessarily must, she is greatly liable to mingle unreasonable prejudices with her calmest deliberations. The action of the South on one point, has placed a weapon in her hands, which she will ever be prompt to wield. I allude to the demand made by public meetings, by the press, and if I mistake not by some legislative assemblies, that the North should stop the discussion of slavery among her own citizens. In this, the South, forgetful of her own prerogatives, made a demand, which she would have indignantly spurned, as an interference with the inalienable rights of freemen. Free discussion is the very foundation on which our liberties are based. If it is the misfortune of the South to be placed in a situation where it will endanger her safety, can she therefore justly require it to be silenced? The principle is one which she would adhere to, as the sole arbiter of her own interests and rights; can she complain if other states and other sections dictate the terms of its being exercised among themselves.

The North will never, unless impelled by influence beyond her present vision, attempt to put down slavery by force. She is too well acquainted with the requirements of reciprocal right, to do a deed which would justify positive interference with her own institutions and usages; but that she will continue to agitate the subject,—to discuss it freely among her own citizens, and to exert an influence prejudicial to slavery, cannot be questioned. It is the very genius of her people to do this. She will exert an influence against all slavery, without design of intermeddling with established customs of any state or government.

In this sense, and to this extent, nearly the whole North are abolitionists; and the difference between the mass of society, and those denominated immediate abolitionists is, that the latter have outrun the former in a sober, rational view of the subject, about as far as a certain father of whom I have heard, that in his overheated zeal for the spiritual welfare of his family threatened *to whip his children if they would'nt pray.* This I consider a fair illustration of the state of public feeling at the North. The great body of the people, although ardently desiring the universal extinction of slavery, and especially in their own country, will join the abolitionists in their measures for its overthrow, about as soon as the rational, intelligent portion of the religious community, although anxiously desiring the salvation of their fellow-men, will adopt the practice of the father above-mentioned.

Thus, I have endeavoured to show the position of the two great sections of our country, as they stand at present with regard to this question. Let us

IV. Secondly, Take a brief view of another mode of adjusting it, viz. *by a dissolution of the Union*. The idea of such a result ought never to be indulged for a moment. But as it has been plainly brought before the public, and as it has been loudly asserted, that its dissolution would be preferable to a constant interchange of reproachful language, and to living in a state of increasing excitability and apprehension; it may be proper to look at some of the evident consequences of such an end to our federal government.

Has any man in his folly ever estimated the *value* of this Union. Surely those men who speak of its dissolution as a desirable event, and who threaten to use their exertions to accomplish it, have no adequate perception of its consequences. The very impudence and folly of their clamor, on a question of such unspeakable magnitude, should cause the community to frown them into silence. For myself, I cannot seriously reflect upon such an event without dismay. And it is not mere pride of country—glorious recollections of the past, nor splendid prospects of national destiny in future—neither is it the exultation of monarchs at the downfall of the only republic, that excites my fears. It is the desolations of home; the severing of strongest ties; the disruption of society; the utter ruin of the fairest portion of the globe, just blooming in its glory, over which I would throw a veil. If this nation is destined to perish, let it share the common lot of others, and die of old age, sunk in luxury and corruption, rather than perish by violence, like a youth in the pride of his strength. In its very location; in the circumstances of its settlement; its independence; and in its unrivalled blessings; it stands on an elevation above all which have preceded it: and if it now perish, like the fabled monster, by tearing out its own bowels, the record of its fate will be the darkest page in the blood-written history of man.

The folly of this estimate is equalled only by another—that of calculating the relative strength of the North and South. Even this has been done—probably, for lack of other employment. That the free states are numerically and physically—in almost all the available resources of a country—superior to the South, will not be doubted; and that in *a good cause*, she might be considered, as far as human judgment can extend, an equal match: but before she engages in this strife, she should hear sermons in all her thousand churches from the words of inspiration—"the race is not to the swift, nor the battle to the strong."

No man can take a comprehensive survey of this great country, without being struck with the conviction, that Divine Providence designed it to be one nation. No other country, possessed by a civilized people, presents the same features. Geographically it is one, and cannot be divided (as slavery would divide it) without opening a door for interminable strife. If slavery is destined to dissolve the Union, the division would probably follow the Potomac (or Mason and Dixon's line), and the Ohio. We will suppose the separation to be amicably effected—the public buildings at Washington sold—the national property, the navy, the debt, the public documents, and the national domain to be divided, and all its present interests fairly adjusted. There is indeed some *common property* belonging to the entire Union, which it would be difficult to divide; but in an affair of such moment, veneration for the past would not offer a Gordian knot of restraint. I allude to the battle-fields of the Revolution, and the memorials of that eventful period. The battle-fields are perhaps nearly equally divided, and each might be content with its share. There is Lexington, and Bunker Hill, and Saratoga, in the North; and Eutaw, and King's Mountain, and Yorktown, in the South. The portrait of the father of his country, and also that of his illustrious French compatriot, which now look down upon the legislative hall of Congress, might be severed, and half given to each section; but as the country had so soon attained to such a pitch of refinement, as to render their wisdom useless, it would be more in character to sell them to the highest bidder, as second-hand rubbish. There are men in Europe who would be proud of the trust of keeping these hallowed memorials from sacrilegious hands; and they might perhaps in some future ages be brought forth to kindle a spirit of liberty, and be the patron saints of freedom, in some colony of a tyrant realm.

The relics in the tomb of Mount Vernon, being exposed to disturbance from their location on the borders of the rival states, should also be expatriated.

The four great pictures which adorn the capitol at present,—belonging, as they do, two to each side, might be given up to their respective sections. The figure of Peace, that most exquisite specimen of art, which salutes the rising day with her ever placid countenance from the front portico, should be crowned with the stars, and wrapped in the stripes of the Union, and burnt by the executioner, —the olive branches torn from the talons of the eagle in the senate hall being used for faggots. The eagle himself, the proper emblem of a great freebooter, should be perched upon the helmet of Mars, and carried in the van, as the presiding genius of each army. In the present national motto " *e pluribus unum*," the last word should be exchanged for " *bellum*," and the *disunion* would be complete.

This vast country then, embracing within its extremities nearly twenty-five degrees of latitude, containing sixteen millions of people, speaking the same language, practising the same customs, and professing the same religion; contains two nations. Their interests, which before were reciprocal, are now, by this act of separation, become dissimilar, and at variance.

As the most favourable view of the case, we will assume that temporary residents in either section are permitted to dispose of their property, and retire; or if they choose, to promise allegiance to the state, and remain. One of the first steps of every independent nation is to provide against aggression, and to protect its own interests; accordingly, a chain of posts is established along the boundary from the Atlantic to the Mississippi; and an armed force quartered in each to prevent smuggling, repel invasion, and keep the peace. Where any man may now travel without notice or observation, no man could then pass without scrutiny or a passport.

The mighty Atlantic, which, like its great Author, is no respecter of persons, but bears on its bosom the people and the productions of all nations, rolls with equal majesty and beneficence the shores of both; and, as it now affords a common channel for promoting prosperity, would then offer equal facilities for international strife. Each nation would struggle to obtain a naval superiority, for the protection of its commerce, and the defence of its maritime border. The communication between the North and South, which is now so extensive, and the source of so much prosperity, would be restricted by the same rules that impede the correspondence of foreign and distant nations. Every cask of rice or barrel of sugar would be taxed in the North; every bale of manufactured goods in the South. Every letter and newspaper in passing over the boundary would be subject to rigid inspection. The great object of each would be to enrich and strengthen itself at the expense of its rival. The inhabitants on opposite sides of the Ohio might kindle a war at any time, by shooting each other across the river for pastime. And the seeds of dissension might be disseminated with the greatest facility, from the fact, that unprincipled men of address and intelligence might pass from one section through the other—the language being the same—and spring a mine among a community reposing in conscious security.

But the source of interminable war, would be the navigation of the Mississippi. There is not perhaps a more powerful and universal trait of national character than a disposition to avail itself of the natural advantages of its situation. And this king of rivers, which, with its thousand arms, drains the fairest portion of the globe, was made to bear, as it now does, the products of that portion on its bosom. The voice of Nature on this subject is too plain to be misunderstood. Natural obstacles, though in part overcome by the art and industry of man, forbid any other outlet with equal facility. A great portion of this valley—and that portion to which the outlet is of most importance—lies on one side of the boundary, and the point of destination, fixed by nature, is on the other. Would the states of the Upper Mississippi submit to be debarred the free use of this natural channel? Would the states of the South permit this great avenue to be common property? The event alone can justify an answer.

In view of all these circumstances and causes of international strife, it may well be inquired how long peace could be maintained between the two sections. History will give us some light on this question, and we need not go back to the states of antiquity for information,—*Christian* history will be sufficient for our purpose. Cite first the records of the middle ages. Read attentively the history of those states which overthrew the empire of the West, and began the present monarchies of Europe; the Goths, Franks, and Lombards, whose meagre annals for several centuries are mostly filled with accounts of royal fratricides and paricides—and they will inform you how long brothers of jealous disposition and rival interests will remain in peace. Ask England, our venerated mother, whose records in the time of the *roses*, will give the most satisfactory evidence on this point; for her throne is as deeply red with fraternal blood as any in Christendom.. It would be needless to multiply inquiries or state suppositions on a subject respecting which the history of all ages concurs with every day's experience of human character. Nothing but Divine interposition could avert the last resort in the case under consideration, even to the period to which we have arrived. It cannot be longer stayed. The war of brothers commences. Mutual jealousies, rivalries, and heartburnings, long cherished in secret, burst forth like the tornado in the summer's calm.

The *cause* of each party is as clear by *right* and *just*, as though written in sunbeams. With mutual horror at such unnatural conduct, each party appeals to Heaven for justice, and for avenging the injured, that is, its own cause. Public supplications are offered in sublime mockery for Divine aid throughout the North and South,—and the sword is let loose.

Hundreds of emissaries from the North, filled with the spirit of evil, elude detection, enter the South, excite the slaves to insurrection, and promise them the estates of their masters. In the mean time the energies of the South are distracted, agitated as she is by a civil and a servile war, her agriculture neglected, and her ports of commerce blockaded. The North is divided by factions; many of her best citizens having ever and utterly opposed this resort to arms. But the clamour of the multitude prevails, and in the excitement of the revolution a brave army is raised to conquer the South. But this army finds a theatre of operations very different from what it expected. The resources of the South are distributed on a plan differing entirely from the North. Instead of the frequent villages and wealthy towns of the latter, it finds abundance of pine woods to plunder, with country mansions scattered all over the country, a mile asunder. As it approaches a large town, a cloud of flame, a miniature Moscow, points out its locality, and covers the retreat of the inhabitants. To the utter surprise of these invaders, they have to contend every step with *slaves*. Individuals and squadrons and regiments of negroes oppose their progress continually, fighting heroically for their native soil. They enfilade the woody passages leading to their masters' dwellings and their own, and, like their brethren in Africa, strike their enemies from the bush. As it pushes onward into the country, a new enemy attacks the army. Disease seizes the unacclimated, and the remnant falls an easy prey. Another is raised, equipped, and marched. During all this time, the arts of peace being exchanged for the excitements and the tumult of war, the manufactories of the North are suspended; her shipping unemployed or captured; her agriculture neglected; her enterprize palzied; and vice and crime are the lessons of her former industrious population.

The great courts of Europe, which have been silent but interested spectators of this scene, now, after the combatants appear to be exhausted, under pretence of reconciling difficulties, become engaged in the strife, assist the weaker sufficient to make it an equal match for the stronger, until both parties are completely prostrated, and the energies of the country are destroyed. These allies, having seized upon the most important stations, garrison them with their own troops, under the double plea of preserving peace, and of remuneration for services rendered; and as for the ruined country, they—

"Leave it alone in its glory."

Taking advantage of its prostrate condition, a dozen young Napoleons aspire to the sovereignty. Each gathers a rabble of lawless followers, and as the country exhibits some symptoms of returning life, after one-half the aspirants are defeated or murdered, the remainder having established some authority in different sections, and the impoverished state willing for repose at any sacrifice, the whole country is divided into half-a-dozen kingdoms, ready, as soon as recovered from the desolating scourge, to renew scenes of conquest and violence.

Such is merely the faint outline of a picture which is impressed upon the mind in contemplating a resort to arms as the final result of this controversy. To fill up the picture, would require a volume devoted to the extreme degree of human madness and suffering. If God, who has been our great benefactor, should ordain us a scourge for our ingratitude, and let loose the spirit of anarchy in our country, the strides we have taken in national power and prosperity would be exceeded only by our rushing downward to ruin.

Thirdly. We have another mode of contemplating the settlement of this question, which promises a happier result. This is by concession and compromise. Against any proposition of this nature, I am aware there are strong feelings and prejudices arrayed from that stubborn independence of our people which arrogates to itself a perfection of wisdom, and professes a readiness to defend its opinions and vindicate its conduct to the last extremity. Some of these prejudices will be noticed in pursuing this inquiry; but it may be sufficient to say here, that there is ground to hope that a spirit of concession may prevail from the fact that individual as well as national interests combine to favour it. Men of the habitual reflection of the American people, will ponder upon the certain consequences of disunion and war, before they consent to engage in the strife. And when each man has looked at the stake he has in the question —his personal interest and safety, his family, his friends, his merchandize, his property—he will ask at what price or sacrifice this threatening calamity can be averted, before he decides to meet it.

And that it is a momentous question is proved from the difficulties which surround it. It is grown so enormous that men know not how to grasp it; but there is some light dawning from the right quarter. There are many slaveholders giving their attention deeply to the subject. I have heard plans proposed for its extinction, which evinced a degree of profound observation and reflection. There are plans in contemplation among slaveholders which are worthy of candid attention, and of encouragement from the free states. It is greatly desirable that some of these men could so far overcome the obstacles and the prejudices of their situation, as to give their thoughts to the public. It would elicit inquiry, and they would find many others seeking for information, to whose minds their suggestions, and the fact that the subject of emancipation was exciting public attention at home, would afford relief and gratification. I know the reply which will be made to this suggestion, viz., that the measures of the abolitionists have entirely precluded any such action among slaveholders at present. That it would be unworthy of the South to make any propositions touching emancipation in any form, while the abolitionists were menacing them with ruin. But from this view of the subject I beg to dissent. It is paying the abolitionists a compliment which they do not deserve. They are but a small fraction of northern society, and shall they suspend and obstruct the action of the community, both North and South, on subjects of national interest? But another reason may be offered why this is the proper time for southern men to offer their plans. The movements of abolitionists have awakened public attention at the North to the subject of slavery, and the majority of the people, although not approving their measures, are inquiring for information, and are just in a position to receive favourably any proposition which, while it exposes the errors and mischiefs of immediate abolition, shall offer some feasible plan for doing away the evil. If no such proposition is offered—if every thing which comes from the South, looks only to the perpetuation of slavery—multitudes of this northern majority will probably either settle down into the unwilling belief, that slavery is an unremediable evil, or will fix their attention and their hopes upon some modification of abolition.

With these views, the writer calls upon the South for such declarations of their wishes and intentions, without compromising their own integrity and honour, or yielding to the fanatical spirit of immediate abolition, as may lead the awakened feeling of the North to adopt measures for preserving the public tranquillity, and calm its agitation by manifesting a disposition to at least investigate the merits of the subject.

And I would not startle the patriotism or self-interest of the reader, in declaring, that by concession or compromise, I avow a firm conviction, that colonization offers the best, the only true plan of bringing this controversy to a happy issue—and of making a freeman of the slave. I am aware that my patriotism and philanthropy will both be called in question for this avowal; but to such persons I have only to say that a candid and thorough investigation of the subject has forced this conviction upon me, in spite of powerful and opposing prejudices. And the deliberate attention of the reader is invited to the facts and the reasons which will now be given for this conviction.

The idea of transporting all the slaves back to Africa, seems at first view utterly chimerical; and so the writer once viewed it. But the work is not beyond the reach of possibility; and the rule of a good man respecting a good work is, if he cannot do all he would, he will do all he can. If we cannot remove all the blacks, certainly we can relieve those portions of the country where slavery is becoming a burden. On this point I should regret not having the aid and co-operation of abolitionists. I know they are capable of exerting a powerful influence in this cause, and am confident that it is a mistaken philanthropy which leads them to oppose it. They have entirely different views of human nature from the mass of men, if they think to elevate the negro to an equality with the whites in this country. And unless they possess the power of foreknowledge, and are acting under the inspiration of what shall be at some future period, it is almost self-evident, that their success in the measures which they now so strenuously urge, will result in the injury of the coloured race, both present and prospective. At least such is the conclusion of the writer, in contemplating this subject, in the light of past experience.

I recollect once suggesting the proposition of purchasing the slaves, for the purpose of emancipating them, to an abolitionist of some notoriety, when he immediately replied—" what! buy stolen property? no, never." To what extent the views of this man are those of abolitionists generally, I know not; but would make a few remarks on this point, for the reflection of all northern men. If the negroes were stolen, the North is at least as deeply implicated in the crime as the South. If there is national dishonour in slavery, the North is a partaker in it. If it is to be blotted out in blood, she will inevitably furnish a share. If emancipation can be amicably effected, she must and ought to bear a part of the burden.

That the subject of colonization emancipation is becoming one of increasing interest, is evident from the fact that some of the slave states have state societies formed for encouraging it, which receive legislative aid. And the time is not distant, when the question of African colonization will be agitated *in the national capitol*. Emancipation must become a subject of national interest, of national deliberation and effort. And I should rejoice, were there such a tone of feeling in the country, expressed through the state legislatures and local assemblies, as should demand of Congress to offer to transport to Africa at the national expense, and provide for their temporary maintenance, all the slaves which should be offered by their masters, and all the indigent free blacks who should offer themselves, to return to their father-land. While these were in progress of removal, another proposition might be made to purchase all that should be offered within a limited price and time. By this means public attention would be drawn to this mode of emancipation, and by their gradual removal the utility and expediency of colonization on a large scale would be tested. Should the current of popular feeling among the blacks be directed strongly into this channel, it would soon break down every barrier, and its force become irresistible. Not only the slave and the indigent freeman, who would be aided in their removal, but the man of property, would be anxious to emigrate to join a community where his respectability and influence would be something more than nominal, and not entirely overshadowed and obscured by his superiors. To this plan, I am aware there are strong objections, but I cannot believe the objectors have deliberately canvassed the subject. The question of colonization has entered into the discussions between the North and South on slavery, and each section has imbibed prejudices against it—the North professing to believe that the South encouraged it from interested motives of making slavery more secure; and the latter jealous of every thing emanating from the North, looked upon it as the incipient movement of a society, whose ultimate object was the overthrow of slavery.

This result has been produced by the abolition excitement, since which, for the reasons just mentioned, the Colonization Society has received less favour from the public, than in the first years of its existence. But whatever may be the fate of this society, the cause is a good one, and must prevail. My belief in its *goodness* is based upon observation of human nature and experience of the past—in its *prevalence,* is founded upon the wisdom, justice, and humanity of my countrymen.

First. The South will not listen a moment to

emancipation in any other mode. Those who are opposed to slavery from principle, and those who would be relieved from it as a burden, look only to colonization for relief. They are certainly the best judges of their situation, both present and prospective, and the opposer of colonization may choose between the practicability of changing the public sentiment of an entire community of millions, and the propriety of co-operating in measures of their own adoption. But this fact of southern opposition to emancipation, except the slaves are sent out of the country, is altogether a secondary consideration in advocating colonization. Even if they should consent to a full and free unconditional abolition, I would still urge colonization upon the negro. I would plead for it then, as I do now, first and chiefly, for the very reason that the immediate abolitionists profess to oppose it; that is, from motives of regard for the welfare of the coloured race. I must acknowledge a full conviction, that it is out of the question to elevate the negro to an equality with the whites in this country. And this conviction is the result of a calm and deliberate consideration of the condition—not of the servile and degraded southern slave—*but of the emancipated blacks and their descendants in the free states.*

I cannot reflect upon this condition, without adopting the language of another—" he can never rise, he is a negro !" In proof of this, go to New England, the land of the pilgrims, the boasted home of Christianity, of good morals, of political freedom, of unfeigned philanthropy, and of charitable institutions. There the slave has been free for near half a century, and what is his condition? Where is his place in the family, even of the parish minister? Where in the church, and at the eucharist? He is a *man*, a man of intelligence, of integrity, of property. But can he vote? Has he any political rights? He has been knocking at your legislative doors repeatedly for redress of grievances, for removal of his disabilities, for equal, *Declaration-of-Independence*, rights and privileges—and the only response he has ever obtained is " you are a negro." His property is taxed, but he has no voice in the taxation—a violation of the very principle for which your and his forefathers dared to resist the power of the mother country. He is a native of the state; and if reputation, industry, and knowledge can make a man respectacle, he is entitled to the appellation: but you trample him under foot, and impart the right of suffrage and citizenship to a degraded, ignorant foreigner, who is in every respect (except the colour of his skin) his inferior. He is subject to the most degraded *caste*. You do not hesitate to come in the closest personal contact with the negro, as a barber, or a body servant, but a Jew would sooner eat pork than you would sit at the same table with him. In this remark I speak of the great body of society. Your daughters would be disgraced in associating with parties of black females. Even now they shudder at the bare idea.

I have before stated that southern men ought never to reproach the North on the subject of amalgamation. May it not be said, with much greater emphasis, that the North should be cautious in reproaching the South for infracting the plain letter of Jefferson's Declaration, by denying the blacks their freedom. The latter openly avow a right to keep them in servitude; the former have granted them a freedom, which at the same time they acknowledge to be counterfeit, by withholding from them those privileges which they themselves consider the essential rights of freemen.

Again. Look at Philadelphia, the boasted city of loving brothers, and of good order. You would not believe, from a knowledge of its past history, or a walk through its quiet streets, that materials for a mob could be found in the whole city and liberties; but even Philadelphia is moved, when the African dares a step above his level. A white and a negro walk the streets of Philadelphia, arm in arm!—will posterity believe it!—and Pennsylvania Hall is fired to see the spectacle.

Take the most respectable coloured person in the community, and what is the current observation respecting him? Why exactly this; that he is very smart *for a negro*. The mere report of an intermarriage between a white and black would throw any city of the North into a ferment.

If this is the condition and the standing of the

negro in the free states fifty years after emancipation, how long a period will be required to place him on a level with the whites? When this question is satisfactorily answered, some opinion may be formed of the time requisite to elevate the southern slave to the same equality.

But, it will be answered, public opinion is wrong in consigning the negro to degradation. Admit it, and what follows? Will the true philanthropist spend his life in fruitless struggles to overcome an unconquerable prejudice against the coloured man; or take advantage of that prejudice to place him in a situation, where he may exert all the faculties of his nature for his own benefit? A sort of infamy is every where attached to a state of slavery, and this with his sable complexion fixes an indelible mark upon the negro, which can never be effaced until human nature is radically changed. This country is not the home of the negro; it never can be.* He may continue to live here, but he can never assert the privileges of a freeman; can never develope his powers. He will always be an outcast, trodden under foot, a hewer of wood and drawer

---

* " You may set the negro free, but you cannot make him otherwise than an alien to the European.—The moderns then, after they have abolished slavery, have three prejudices to contend against, which are less easy to attack and far less easy to conquer, than the mere fact of servitude;—the prejudice of the master, the prejudice of the race, and the prejudice of colour."

DE TOCQUEVILLE, *Democracy in America.*

of water. He has no better inheritance in prospect for his children, than to be servants of servants. In view of this nearly universal prejudice, many of the best men of the North are decidedly in favour of colonization; and I doubt not also the greater portion of the community who have soberly investigated the subject.

And here the opposer alike of colonization and slavery will inquire, why not free the slave, and let him remain as a hired servant? I answer, chiefly for the reasons just stated. This plan offers at first view a very plausible mode for extinguishing slavery, and elevating the negro, and as such deserves attention. I have ever believed that if the South would adopt it, it would relieve her from very great present embarrassments. The negro would have a motive to labour, to exercise frugality and economy, which he cannot have in his present state. If the planter should divide his cultivated fields among his labourers, and offer a premium for the greatest product, he would realize a larger profit. The fear of insurrection, a suspicion of which now makes every man's ear to tingle, would be entirely removed. The resources of the whole South would no doubt be greatly increased.

But I am aware that the South looks upon this proposition as one bearing the impress of folly upon its very face, and giving rise to no emotions but those of contempt and ridicule. Perhaps the best men would reject it instantly. The whole South would reject it unanimously. Nevertheless this fact does not alter my opinion. I cannot believe it a futile project, until the experiment shall have been tried. But still its ultimate results —taking the experience of the North, and a knowledge of human nature for our guides—are far from being clear or satisfactory. Certainly, I should not hesitate to declare a preference for colonization, in comparison with this plan. The one offers certain advantages for the negro, the other must be comparatively a doubtful experiment. It has been shown, what is the present condition of the blacks in the free states—that their freedom is merely nominal; and from that we may form an opinion of the slow progress which the blacks of the South would make in improving themselves.

In considering this point, we must not lose sight of the agents by which this change is to be effected. If the slaves are emancipated, the act must be done by southern legislators. Suppose for a moment they consent to try the experiment of emancipating the slaves without removing them. He has studied human character to very little purpose, who does not at once perceive that in the steps preliminary to this event, effectual measures for self-defence would be taken. Various enactments would be made with reference to the probable consequences of such an event; and one not the least important would have a direct bearing upon the political rights of the blacks. Would the right of suffrage be extended to them, or would this prerogative of freemen be fenced around with so many barriers, that but few of them would be able to surmount them for generations. The laws would most certainly be so framed as to exclude them forever, if possible, from any share in state or national legislation. Were the right of suffrage given them to the same extent that is now practised in some of the free states, they would control every department of government in more than one of the slave states, at the very next following election. And I need not ask, what southern, but what northern legislator would consent to occupy a seat in the representative hall with a negro! The consequence of such freedom as they would obtain, would be, either a degraded state of inferiority—or if the blacks should increase faster than the whites (a very probable supposition), they would soon be in a condition to demand equal rights.

But again; these slaves are set free, exceedingly ignorant, totally destitute of property. Accustomed to entire direction in all their employments, they are now cast off, and told to provide for themselves. They have nothing to commence with, no houses, lands, tools, or trades; and though used to labour, very few of them have sufficient intelligence to direct their labours to a useful purpose or a profitable result. Would not a community of whites in such circumstances be satisfied with the gross indulgences of sensual propensities, and drag out a miserable existence rather as brutes than as men. What then can be hoped from the negro, who, in addition to his exertions for personal advantage in the most unfavourable circumstances, has to combat every step with an unconquerable prejudice against his colour, deepened by a recollection of his late servile condition. To the prejudice which now consigns him to a secluded degradation in the intelligent, enlightened free states, would be added a strong, ever wakeful suspicion at the South, arising from the physical inequality of the blacks.

In view of these almost certain results, I cannot perceive how the friend of the African race can wish him to remain in this country as a freeman. Great rejoicings have been made in some parts of the country, at the emancipation of the slaves in the British colonies in our neighbourhood. I shall be glad, if these rejoicings do not prove to be premature. Every good man and friend of his race, must rejoice at the abandonment or extinction of slavery, wherever it offers a prospect of improving the condition of the slave; and every such man *will* believe that freedom is preferable to slavery in every case, until observation and experience disprove the fact. Very contradictory reports have been published respecting the operation of the apprenticeship system, and abolition in the British islands; but sufficient has been elicited to convince the writer of the following facts:—That full emancipation is safe for the master—that the negro slave is the same passive machine in Jamaica as in the southern states, and that he is looked upon as the same degraded inferior—that continual altercation will arise between the employer and the hireling in such cases respecting wages—and that the latter has little to hope from his late master, in aiding his improvement in any respect. The consequences of this measure cannot be known with certainty any faster than time develops them, although it will, no doubt, eventually tend to the improvement of the negro. We should, however, be cautious in all our speculations on this subject, and especially in comparisons between the state of these colonies and our own country. The former are not independent states, but entirely under the control of the British crown or Parliament; consequently the government of England not only dictates the time and mode of emancipation, but the condition of the freedmen with regard to citizenship. The present popular feeling of the British nation indicates that this will be favourable to the negro. In view of these facts there can be little doubt that one result of colonial emancipation will be an ultimate abandonment of the island to the blacks, unless the whites should choose to live under their legislative control.

VII. But there is a better prospect for the slave in the land of his fathers. Tropical Africa appears to be the home destined by the Creator for the negro, and has been the residence of his race, from time immemorial. There is room enough even in the vicinity of the coast of Upper Guinea for all the black population of the Union; as but a very small part of its luxuriant soil has been brought under cultivation. There the negro can stand erect in his manhood, and, in the face of his brother, behold only an equal. No master has power to task him, or make him feel continually a consciousness of bitter degradation. He may there assert the rights and dignity of a freeman, and cultivate the faculties which God has given him. If he has enterprize, there is a sufficient field for its exercise in the unknown regions of his father-land. If he has learned any thing valuable, in his state of vassalage, he can there turn it to his own advantage. If he is capable of exciting an influence upon Africa in favour of Colonization and Christianity, she needs it all. His religion, his character, his intellect, are here thrown into the shade, by his white superiors; there they may be exerted for his own benefit, and the improvement of his benighted countrymen. Here, in the most favourable circumstances, he obtains but a partial reward for his labour—he is surrounded by an influence which neutralizes his utmost exertions—there, he has to compete only with equals, and may obtain a reward bounded only by the limits of his industry, his enterprize, and skill. His employments here are the same which will be in request there. Here he cultivates the earth, and another enjoys the harvest. There he may survey his cotton or cane-field with a conscious pride of feeling that the fruits of his toil are all his own. The products of his country will find a ready market, and he may even come in competition with his old master in producing the staple articles of commerce. Even now the coffee of Liberia is in demand through the Union. Her cotton, sugar, and rice are of the best quality, and there is no question but she may cultivate all the productions of the tropics, including the teas, the spices, the dyeing vegetables, and the drugs of India. Of the finest fruits she has a profusion almost without cultivation, equal to any other section of the globe.

But, it will be answered, the climate of tropical Africa is unhealthy for immigrants. This is undoubtedly true. It is a well known fact that emigrants from a northern to a southern climate, or from an old settled to a new country, must go through a process of acclimation, in which more or less die. This is abundantly evident, from the progress of population in our own country. But from impressions on my own mind, without reference to tabular statements, I am decidedly of opinion that the coloured emigrants to Liberia have enjoyed greater immunity from fatal diseases than emigrants from one part of our own country to another. The mortality among them has been incomparably less than among the first settlers of Plymouth or Jamestown: and I doubt not a less proportion of American emigrants die in Liberia, than of slaves who are carried from the northern slave states to the southern, or of white emigrants from the eastern states to the western country.

Those who doubt the correctness of this statement are invited to furnish the facts, and give, in tabular form, the data from which a comparison may be made. It is, if I mistake not, generally admitted that Liberia is a very healthy country for the natives, and as much so at least, as tropical climates generally to foreign residents of temperate habits. A large majority of the whites who have gone there, and resided more than a year in the service of the Colonization Society, have survived, although many of them were from the northern states of this country. A number of these were in this country during the last year, and their evidence on the subject is entirely worthy of credit. But so important a point as healthfulness of the climate should be duly weighed in connection with the removal of a numerous population; and whoever, on either side, should make wanton mistatements on this subject to favour the designs of a party, can be looked upon in no other light than a trifler with human existence.

Does not America owe it to Africa, to send back her children, and their descendants. We have used them as servants for nearly two centuries, and have made them no equivalent. If they have become wiser, it has been accidental, not a positive gift. They have engrafted some of our worst vices on their own. Our forefathers were among the first who engaged in the horrible traffic of slaves, and were thus guilty, in a great measure, of exciting those murderous wars, which have torn and scourged that unhappy country for ages. We may pay the debt in part by returning those over which we have control; by placing them in happier circumstances, and making the settlements a barrier to the coast trade in slaves. And as the whole nation is guilty in this matter, and as the whole, also, has been profited by the toil of the slave, his redemption and welfare becomes an object of national importance. Not until the nation becomes interested in the subject, will the work be accomplished. It is too vast, too burdensome, to be effected by an individual, a society, or a state. And the resources of the country are equal to the mighty enterprize. Has not God been our benefactor to put into our hands the means of paying this enormous debt. He has given us peace (with very slight intermissions) from the commencement of our national existence, and multiplied our riches without measure. The whole period of fifty years, has been one scarcely interrupted scene of onward, onward increase and prosperity, heretofore unknown in the annals of the world. Our population has quadrupled, our means increased a hundred fold. I cannot review this scene of progressive welfare without a conviction that God intends a great offering shall be made, to remove from our midst an entire people, by whose burdens this great accumulation has in part, been produced. We stand in relation to the Africans, as the Egyptians stood to Israel; and as sure as the latter were liberated, so surely must these be released. It is needless to go into the evidences of this coming event. They are distinctly perceptible to every Christian, and philanthropist, and patriot. The great question is, shall we come forward as a people, and make the time and mode of their discharge a great thank offering, becoming the magnanimity of a nation which is above the fear of an outward foe; or shall we grasp the possession, as the lion grasps the lamb, until the decree for emancipation shall be executed *after* suffering all the plagues of Egypt. And the real philanthropist is equally confident of the ultimate redemption of the slave, and the necessity of sending him home to Africa. He must needs go back, not only for his own welfare, but for enlightening his countrymen. The day is dawning, in which Ethiopia is to be civilized and Christianized.

And although this undertaking appears so vast, and apparently unattainable, its difficulties will gradually disappear when the work is commenced in earnest. When this shall be done, there will be less want of means than of willingness to apply them. The resources of the nation are annually accumulating far beyond what would be required for this object, by the most ardent and active interest in its accomplishment. We have presented the singular spectacle of a nation, receiving more revenue than it knew what to do with; and with prudence and integrity in the national councils, such a period is before us again. The very operation of our present national system and laws, will produce such a result continually, while we have wisdom to keep in peace with the nations. Either of two items of the national revenue, that from the customs or the public lands, would be sufficient to effect this great work in a progressive manner. Will this application, so equal, so little burdensome, so just, and for the accomplishment of so important an object, be denied? And will not the nation demand that the navy be enlisted in and devoted to this great work? The ships of war, which are now decaying in the harbours, and the gallant men who are rusticating on shore for want of employment on the ocean, should be engaged in this business, greatly to reduce the expense, and to benefit the service. By the agency of this single power, as many might be transported (at the least expense) as could be advantageously settled in Africa for some years to come. And it would be a spectacle worthy of our infant but energetic Union, to see the ocean covered with American vessels, as transports and convoys, carrying back to their father-land, that portion of our population which is extensively regarded by some of the most enlightened nations as a dark spot upon our national character. The songs of a nation redeemed, swelling over the ocean, would be re-echoed with great joy, by all human intelligence. Such a spectacle would show to the admiration of the world, that the boasted motto of our statesmen and ambassadors—" equal and exact justice to all men"—is not an unmeaning or false declaration, and would elevate us in the estimation of the wise and good, more than the gaining of a hundred battles, or the exhibition of Roman valour.

By engaging in this enterprize on a scale suited to its magnitude, treaties would be entered into with native tribes, and cessions of territory required, by which we should check and assist to extinguish the merciless slave trade; a work in which our government has but slightly co-operated, from motives of national policy, on which I need not animadvert. With the reputation and the resources of the nation to sustain it, this undertaking should not be carried on in a parsimonious manner. The negro should not be sent empty away. The destitute should be provided with homes, and every family a lot in proportion to its numbers, that they might in reality sit under their own vine and fig tree.

The accomplishment of this enterprize, or even its vigorous commencement, would form an era in the history of Africa, and its influence could not be otherwise than salutary. These ransomed servants would carry the Bible and the Christian ministry along with them, and churches and schools would be established in all their borders. It would be a land of Goshen, not like that of old; but the light in their dwellings would shine afar, and illuminate the gross darkness of that mighty continent. The news of their coming would be spread abroad, and barbarian kings from the vast interior would send messengers to hold " palaver " with the Christian foreigners. Their example might teach these rude nations, that the arts of peace were preferable to the horrors of war. With wise governors and counsellors to mould the infant state; with a sufficient number of workmen in the useful arts; with the blessings of Christianity and civilization; it would possess advantages, which few incipient colonies ever enjoyed. By its industry, and enterprize, in developing its agricultural resources, this infant nation would repay in a few generations all the burdens imposed by its establishment in its contributions to American commerce.

To those who shrink from the contemplation of this project—the purchase and transportation of the slaves—in view of the expense, let me suggest a reflection for my countrymen on the objects for which enormous sums of money are now expended by the nation. I will instance only one, the Florida war. It is painful to reflect upon the insatiability of a false national honour. The sum which has been expended, estimated at $20,000,000, in combating a handful of Indians without subduing them, would purchase a territory in Africa large enough for all the black population in the Union, and build them houses to live in; or a thousandth part of it would have secured the friendship of these savages, instead of making them inveterate enemies.

But the national honour was said to be in jeopardy; and to sustain this, the people have as yet quietly submitted to this enormous expense. But if national renown has any connection with the prodigal expenditure of money, we shall have a niche in the temple of glory. Future history will secure us the undying fame of putting forth the energies of a mighty nation against fifteen hundred rude barbarians, and killing them at an expense of fifty thousand dollars per head. Fifty odd millions more will extinguish the tribe, unless, as in mercantile affairs, the capitation value should be increased as the number is lessened. But even if the recent project of building a wall of living men across the peninsula, to repress their incursions, should succeed, and no more millions be demanded at present—the glory of the past is at least secure, and we may be assured that posterity *will do us justice*. I regret to mar the joy of this prospective fame, by suggesting that the price of killing one Indian would have given a new and happier life to a hundred negroes. But Indians and negroes are very different men, and national honour and national benevolence are at present far from being convertible terms.

VIII. In closing this appeal, the writer begs serious attention to the following remarks, as a suitable appendix to the subject. It has been hinted, that emancipation must become a subject of national interest and effort. On this point I am satisfied that reflection and discussion will produce a degree of unanimity as to the fact, however the people may disagree respecting the extent and application of the national resources. There is a tone of independent feeling and action in the South, which in two or three states has already begun the work of Colonization, and when fully awakened, will go far towards effecting the object; but even should state action be sufficient for the purpose, the interposition of government would be required in directing their plans to unity of design. Unless the national standard should he raised in Africa, and a governor or board of control have supreme jurisdiction, petty jealousies would break out into anarchy and collisions between the emigrants and colonial governments of the different states, and thus all the great objects of Colonization would be defeated. There can be little doubt that when the current of popular feeling on this subject shall run in the proper channel, it will give the helm of direction to the national legislature. The popular will is the supreme dictator, the federal government is its agent. The great object at present should be to diffuse information. There are powerful influences already at work, and if the opposing sentiments are left to combat in open field, the truth will be elicited by their collision. Nothing can be effected now, but an appeal to the good sense and sober judgment of the people, for there is no room for its admission into legislation. There is a struggle too engrossing, between the ins and outs of party, to listen to matters of purely benevolent import. It is the curse and disgrace of our country, that the demon of party feeling and party interest sits enthroned in the capital,—and not only in the capital, but the state governments. Every where the predominant party stretches its prerogative to the utmost. No influence is allowed to the minority, no patriotism recognized, although it constitutes perhaps nine-twentieths of the people; no personal reputation, no amount of public service can shield the man from proscription and obloquy, who does not fall down and worship the great idol of party. Legislation seems to be not for the nation, but for the party. The very spirit which actuates a victorious army, maddened by an obstinate conflict, to rush onward over a beaten and retiring foe, appears to govern our political and legislative action. Perhaps the reader may suppose these remarks to be levelled at the present administration. It is difficult to decide which side is the most deserving. The spirit manifested by the opposition gives but too much evidence, that its first acts of power would be exercised in effacing every vestige of the present party domination. The writer is no party follower. If he loves Cæsar less, it is because he loves Rome more.

There are indeed some appeals to patriotic principles, some assertion of independent thought in the debates of the capitol; but the loaves and fishes of office are evidently the great object of patriotic ardor. And it is loudly proclaimed by the clamorous patriots of the leading presses on both sides, that the very hope of freedom depends upon the success of their doctrines and measures. A wise man of old had these very Solomons in mind, when he said "truly ye are the men, and wisdom shall die with you." The government is yet in the hands of the people. If they have not sufficient virtue and knowledge to retain it, they will be the first to feel the weight of anarchy and despotism. If they permit their eyes to be blindfolded, and themselves led by those whom they sustain and support, they cannot complain if they are brought to the very brink of the precipice. In the present state of the public mind, there is little room for the exercise of patriotic benevolence. Amid the storm and tumult of partizan rancor, the welfare of the slave or the interest of his master, are subjects of secondary importance. Even should the question be now agitated as one having a national bearing, it would be swallowed up in the vortex of party. The lover of his country and his fellow-men, can only exert an individual influence in endeavouring to diffuse facts, and awaken a spirit of inquiry; leaving to Infinite Wisdom to curb the elements of discord and party selfishness; and bring about a period, when men shall live and act for the well-being of their fellow-men.

CONCLUSION.

In revising this brief work for the press, after several months' delay since it was first written, the writer begs the indulgence of the reader in offering a few additional observations, and making some explanatory remarks to prevent misapprehension.

First, however, he would state that a more careful observation, and a more extended survey of the whole field of controversy, including a somewhat enlarged acquaintance with abolition periodicals—although residing himself among a slave community—have resulted in a stronger conviction that the positions laid down, and the facts stated in this work, are in the main, correct. In expressing his views in the foregoing pages, the writer is not aware of being influenced by any sinister motives, nor can he, on the other hand, lay claim to any very excitable feelings of complacency, in prospect of receiving the flattering encomiums of any party, to which these pages are particularly addressed. He never asked himself respecting any thing he was about to write, "what will slaveholders say to this?" or "how will abolitionists relish that?" He has expressed his own opinions, and aimed at stating facts without regard to fear or favour of any man or body of men. He never was a member of any society, having any connection with the question of slavery, nor did he take any person's counsel with regard to the propriety of what he was about to write. The impressions made on his mind, by a slight acquaintance with practical slavery, induced a wish to throw some light on the vexed and agitated subject; and when this wish began to assume a tangible form in writing, the great and important inquiry,—"what do truth, and justice, and future accountability require?" was kept continually in view. That strong language has been frequently used, and that the free states have received a large share of pointed rebuke in the foregoing pages, is freely admitted: that the sentiments addressed to any section or class of the community, are more severe than truth and facts will warrant, will be cheerfully acknowledged, *on conviction*. The writer claims no exemption from the frailties or infirmities of humanity—he only bespeaks the indulgence of wiser men, that the errors of the head may not be imputed to the heart.

That his inquiries and observations should result in recommending Colonization was entirely unforeseen at the commencement. He once laughed at the impracticable scheme, and, with a good portion of the *abolition prejudice* against it, set it down as an enterprize, something worse than visionary. But a candid view of *both sides* of the question, and a deliberate survey of the whole controversy, has resulted in an entire conviction that this plan offers the only feasible, benevolent, effectual remedy for American slavery. Were his circumstances such as to warrant the undertaking, he would willingly devote his humble efforts, to persuading and assisting the injured and degraded coloured population of the free states, to go back to the home of their fathers. He knows of no field, in which true benevolence could be more usefully employed.

Again, the writer is aware that he will be charged by the spirit of modern abolition, with feeling a strong sympathy for slaveholders. In one sense he pleads guilty to this charge; and he is confident a large number of abolitionists would do the same, if they were *acquainted* with slavery. He would vindicate slaveholders, when they are traduced—when arraigned before a tribunal to which they owe no submission,—and when the misdeeds of a fraction are imputed to the whole body. Beyond this, the charge cannot be substantiated. If denounced as a defender of "horrible cruelty," or even wishing to perpetuate slavery, I would only answer, " it is a small thing to be judged of man's judgment." But I am frank to declare, that the more slavery and abolition are brought into contrast, the more I am convinced there are *two sides* to the question. Are not the abolitionists aware that slaves were bought and sold and advertised in Boston as *common occurrences,* before the Revolution—and that when it was abolished, or about to be abolished, many slaves were carried from the North and *sold* to the southern planters, to *save a loss?* Do not they very well know that slavery was forced upon the colonies by the mother country, and one of the colonial assemblies sharply rebuked, (and *its petitions rejected*), for remonstrating against it. But they will say, "we have now abolished it entirely:" true, and presuming upon the act, you are now saying in effect—" stand by, for I am holier than thou." This spirit will never effect peaceable emancipation.—Neither will the good sense of the community ever resolve to pull down slavery, because there are bad men, monsters, engaged in it. After publishing the horrible atrocities of the system in their periodicals for years, the abolitionists have collected the whole series into one volume, with large additions, to " astound" the people with the horrid cruelties of slavery. This volume contains the evidence of a " thousand witnesses.'i Are the slaveholders of thirteen states to be denounced as out of the pale of humanity, by these thousand witnesses? Suppose some one should bring the testimony of a thousand witnesses to prove that slaveholders were kind, humane, and indulgent?—would abolitionists allow the testimony on one side, as an offset to the other? But again, say the abolitionists,—" human nature is so bad, that where men have the power of slaveholders, the *will* abuse it." Let us apply this argument to another subject. Human nature loves rum so well, that wherever men can get it, they *will* drink to excess. And would the people of New England quietly submit to the insinuation, that the whole mass of society were drunkards, because a thousand witnesses had testified that they had seen beastly intoxication in various parts of New England? Dr. Johnson said, the man who was continually declaring that all men were rogues, incontestibly proved that one at least was so. And I will venture to suggest, even at the hazard of being called an advocate of slavery, that there is some negative good at least in the restraints of slavery. Abolitionists know very well what numbers of free blacks at the North are miserable drunkards. *There are very few such among slaves*, chiefly because they are slaves. But multitudes of free blacks in the slave states are like those just mentioned at the North, a burden to themselves and a nuisance to society.

In conclusion, I will venture to propose to abolitionists, how they may effect abolition. Slavery is at best an untenable position if rightly approached. But the abolitionists have hitherto attacked it in their own strength—and have failed. They are at present "a house divided against itself." They have in several instances urged on their followers to the polls,—and have failed. They have endeavoured to unite the people of the free states in their plans and measures—and have failed. Let them undertake to conquer slavery, as the apostles undertook to conquer the world,—and they will succeed. Had the disciples remained in Judea, lecturing the Jews upon the abominations and cruelties of heathen idolatry, how soon would such measures have converted Greece, and Rome, and Scythia? But they took their lives in their hands, and went forth to preach to the idolater. I can assure the abolitionists, there are large "fields, white, and ready for the harvest," at the South. In many of these fields, the masters acknowledge the evil of slavery, and are anxiously looking for relief. They now consider abolitionists —and with too much reason—as incendiaries and fanatics. But under the influence of that spirit and power which accompanied the apostles, the chains would imperceptibly loosen and fall from the slave. The master cannot withstand such a spirit. Go entirely defenceless, trusting in the arm of the Almighty. "He that takes the sword shall fall by the sword." Put the slaveholder upon his conscience. Hitherto you have put him entirely upon his legal rights, and there he is strong. Have you not men for this service? Men with the New Testament in their hands, and its spirit in their hearts? No other spirit can subvert slavery, so as to bring good out of the evil. Slavery cannot be *forced* down, without deeply injuring both master and slave. Even should the measures of abolitionists succeed, and the servants remain on the soil, they will be but servants still, and will need the goodwill and friendship of their employers. If they should be induced to go to Africa, the assistance and counsel of their masters will be a source of gratification and prosperity.

It becomes the intelligence, the justice, and the Christianity of the North to send men, in whom the public can confide, to the South, to bring back an accurate report of what slavery is practically, before judgment is made up respecting it. Thus far the statements on the subject have been of an *ex parte* character. I do not believe the people of the South would object to have slavery examined by men of principle and intelligence. Openness of conduct is a strong trait in their character. They would submit to it with as good a grace at least as the people of the North would to an examination of their civil and domestic customs and usages.

Although the fact may be of no interest to the public, the writer claims a pride of country as an

American, not exceeded by that of any of his cotemporaries. And his pride is, not to be a northern or a southern man, but an American. His vision is not confined to a state or section, but embraces the country—the whole country. When the bond of union is loosened, and falls to pieces, the charm of American citizenship will be broken. As the first independent nation on this side the Atlantic, we have preserved the continental title, and if true to ourselves we shall sustain a reputation worthy of the name. Unless we cherish a national, an American feeling, we shall lose or become unworthy the great name we have assumed, and which is recognized throughout the world. As soon as sectional or selfish interests shall have triumphed, and rent the Union in pieces, petty appellations will be attached to petty sovereignties. There will be none worthy the names of Americans; and a New Yorker, or a Carolinean, will take rank with a Brazilian, or a Guatimalean. Every American should cherish this national feeling with the spirit of a man who stands as a connecting link in a line of illustrious men, whose worth and reputation he is to transmit to posterity.

With these views, and apprehending a fatal issue to the Union from this cause, were my voice of sufficient influence to be heard, I would summon an assembly of the free states, to discover, as accurately as possible, the state of public sentiment, and to offer to the South some plan for the extinction of slavery, in the spirit of sympathy and generosity, and propose to co-operate in the work. Could I, on the other hand, gain the ear of the South, I would call on her citizens for an explicit avowal of their views of slavery, soliciting them to state the terms on which they would accede to the wishes of the North, and the sacrifices they would make for national union. Should these efforts fail to settle the controversy, I would exhort each to resist to the utmost every attempt to stir up sectional strife,—to bear and forbear with all long suffering, rather than consent to a civil convulsion, leaving to the judgment of a wiser generation, and the guidance of Divine Providence, the future settlement of the question.

With respect to the manner of this performance, the writer would bespeak the indulgence of critical readers. It was written during such brief and irregular intervals, as could be spared from a very laborious and harassing employment—without opportunity to study connection of parts, or make it critically conformable to the rules of rhetoric and grammar. Without entering into any laboured argument, the writer has aimed chiefly to throw together statements, and facts, and opinions on the principal subjects of controversy, in a manner intelligible to the great body of the community. Perhaps he has offered nothing new. If so, he can only plead the scarcely pardonable excuse of good intentions, in adding to the great mass of useless publications. If he has merely suggested some ideas worthy of being transplanted from a barren into a better soil, where they may flourish, and bring forth good fruit, his labour will not be altogether in vain.

District of Columbia, June, 1839.

THE END.

Soc
E
449
I58
1971